springtime for
YOUR SPIRIT

springtime for YOUR SPIRIT

90 Devotions of Hope, Joy & New Beginnings

MICHELLE MEDLOCK ADAMS
& ANDY CLAPP

Good Books

New York, New York

Good Books books may be purchased in bulk
at special discounts for sales promotion, cor-
porate gifts, fund-raising, or educational purposes. Special editions can also be created to
specifications. For details, contact the Special
Sales Department, Good Books, 307 West 36th
Street, 11th Floor, New York, NY 10018 or
info@skyhorsepublishing.com.

Good Books is an imprint of Skyhorse
Publishing, Inc.®, a Delaware corporation.

Visit our website at www.goodbooks.com.

10 9 8 7 6 5 4 3 2 1

Library of Congress Cataloging-in-Publication
Data is available on file.

Cover design by David Ter-Avanesyan
Cover photograph by Shutterstock

Interior by Amber Weigand-Buckley and
Alexander Turner #barefacedcreativemedia.
Photos copyright © by Canva and Unsplash.

Edited by Nicole Frail

Print ISBN: 978-1-68099-775-0
Ebook ISBN: 978-1-68099-776-7

Printed in China

For my sister, Martie Medlock Spaulding.
I am so grateful that God gave me you as
my big sissy. Just like Springtime brings the
sunshine back to Indiana, your very presence lights up a room, Mart. You are called
for such a time as this. Love you!
— Michelle "Missy" Medlock Adams

To Coach Biles,
You touched my life and made me believe
I could do anything in life. You fought for
me when I needed someone to stand up and
fight. Thank you for those marvelous Spring
memories of tennis courts, overcoming obstacles, and learning how to win at life.
— Andy Clapp

ACKNOWLEDGMENTS FROM MICHELLE

I want to thank my wonderful agent, Cyle Young, for always believing in me and encouraging me when I have my "crazy writer moments." I'm so grateful for you and for my Serious Writer family. I love that we get to "do life" together.

I'm grateful to Pastor Andy Clapp, my coauthor on this devotional. You are without a doubt the most amazing representation of humility and service to others that I've ever encountered. You always go the extra mile for people, spreading the love of Jesus everywhere you go. (We need to make bracelets that say "WWAD"—What Would Andy Do?)

And, to my amazingly patient and wonderful husband, Jeff, for always being my biggest cheerleader and encouraging me to do what God has called me to do. I'm so thankful for you and the way that you love me. I am one blessed woman.

And, lastly, to my Heavenly Father . . . for without You, God, I would be lost. Thank You, Lord, for saving me, for loving me unconditionally, and for all of the many blessings You've given me. You are an awesome God.

ACKNOWLEDGMENTS FROM ANDY

Andy would like to thank his family for all of their support. He also wishes to thank Michelle Medlock Adams for this opportunity to work together and his church, Mt. Zion Baptist Church, for their unwavering support. He appreciates you, the reader, and is eternally thankful to his agent, Cyle Young, the Serious Writer family, and his former tennis coach, Kevin Biles. Thank you to Nicole Frail for your support and help on this project and thank you to all of those who have taught at Writer's Conferences such as Blue Ridge, Florida Christian Writers Conference, and the North Carolina Christian Writers Conference. So many people have poured into this work and for each one, Andy is forever grateful.

table of contents

"I've learned that no matter what happens, or how bad it seems today, life does go on, and it will be better tomorrow."

MAYA ANGELOU

MICHELLE

new growth,
NEW SEASON

"THAT WAS REALLY GOOD TODAY," I SAID TO MY OLDER SISTER AS SHE FINISHED TEACHING THE ONLINE BIBLE STUDY WE'D BEEN SHARING ON FACEBOOK. "WANT TO GO TO LUNCH?"

"Sure," she said, grabbing her purse.

It had only been about three months since my brother-in-law passed away from COVID. It was unexpected, and horrible, and heartbreaking. My sister had been very strong throughout the entire ordeal, but I knew losing her precious husband was the most devastating thing she'd ever faced. As we headed out her front door, my sister gasped.

"Look," she said, pointing to the little green sprouts, barely visible, next to her front steps. "My hostas are coming back!"

I squinted. "Yes, I see them! I think we can officially say that Spring has sprung," I joked.

"It's about time," she said.

I could hear the emotion in her voice. Winter 2020 had been colder and darker on so many levels. We not only craved Spring; we desperately needed it. We needed to see new growth poking through the ground. We needed to feel the warmth of sunshine on our faces. We needed to hear the birds chirping. We needed it all. Of course, none of those things would bring back my brother-in-law, but the changing of seasons brought with it the promise of better days ahead. And every day since the afternoon those little hostas made their appearance has seemed a bit brighter and more hopeful.

If 2020 has taught us anything, it's taught us that life is precious, that every moment is a gift, and that Jesus is still good in the midst of bad times.

Just like those little hostas that were dormant for a season and sprang to life at the appointed time, so will we. If you're having a hard time right now; if you've recently suffered a great loss; or if you're still in that dormant season—hang in there. Know this—God hasn't forgotten you, and He is right there with you through every season. Remember, we often grow the most during those dormant times so trust the process and hold onto the hope you have in Jesus. Your Springtime is coming.

plant the Word—

"For I am about to do something new. See, I have already begun! Do you not see it? I will make a pathway through the wilderness. I will create rivers in the dry wasteland." (Isaiah 43:19, NLT)

pray the Word—

Thank You, God, for loving me and sticking by me through every season. Help me to trust You even when I can't see anything but darkness. Help me to have faith even when I can't feel Your presence. And help me, Lord, to be sensitive to others who might be experiencing loss. Let me show them Your love. Amen.

work the Word—

Do you know someone who is suffering great loss right now? It's difficult to know what to do or say when someone you love is grieving, but experts agree on a few helpful things you can do.

- Rather than say the generic, "Call if there's anything I can do," make a specific offer to help. For example, say: "Could I go grocery shopping for you?" or "Would it be helpful if I stopped by and did some cleaning for you?"

- Rather than ask the standard, "How are you?" which will probably generate the automatic (but nonauthentic) response, "I'm fine," ask: "Are you sleeping at night?" or "Are you overwhelmed with visitors?" Or "Would you like some company?"

- Most importantly, don't just say, "I'm praying for you," in a flippant way. Actually take the time to pray for that person every single day. You might even ask if they would like you to pray with them at that very moment.

DID YOU KNOW?

Psalms 56:8, NLT, says: "You keep track of all my sorrows. You have collected all my tears in your bottle. You have recorded each one in your book." That verse really shows us that God has compassion and mercy toward His children, and that's us! He knows about every tear you've ever cried, and He cares. Why not let your Heavenly Father love on you today? Just bask in His promises for a bit.

doggone,
THOSE DOGWOODS

WINTER'S BLAND GIVES WAY TO SPRING'S BEAUTY.

Before Spring, all but the evergreens blend in with one another. The barren branches speak of the death of what was. What began so beautifully the previous spring became the brown drab of the winter. But a new season has come.

In North Carolina, our state flower is the flowering of the dogwood tree. Every Spring, the beauty of life in the dogwoods overtakes what appeared dead before. The white blooms create a breath-taking view.

Along my drive to church, a house captures my attention. The long driveway to the house features nothing but a line of dogwoods, their splendor noted by all who pass by. Twenty dogwoods announce that a new season dawns and the majesty of a new scenery gives hope.

The first time we drove past, I told my wife and kids, "Doggone! Look at those dogwoods. Isn't that just beautiful?" My little girls gave "oohs" and "ahhs" as their little eyes absorbed what they hadn't seen before. Crystal, my wife, just smiled and stared.

"The blooming of these trees reminds us of the beauty of forgiveness," a pastor once told me. "What was ugly before is wrapped in beauty, just as we are when we are covered in His righteousness." Those words echo in my ear each time I pass that house during the Spring.

The work of God brings such a view to life. His working underneath what is seen leads to awe when it comes into plain sight. Such is a truth of the work of forgiveness in our lives.

The ugliness of our sin tarnishes our lives. Sin leaves us barren and brown, appearing as if we are lifeless. Sin robs our lives of the beauty that God created us to hold. Yet, a new season awaits our lives.

But God.

As Paul explained, Jesus, who knew no sin, took on our sin. He carried the guilt, the shame, and the ugliness of it all. What do we receive in return? Paul says that Jesus became sin so we could be wrapped in His righteousness.

With a turn to Jesus, a prayer for forgiveness, and a commitment to Him, a new life begins. Though unseen to begin with, the new life of Christ begins to bud from within and the ugliness of before is overtaken by the beauty of righteousness. When the Lord sees us, He no longer sees the sin or the dirtiness of before. When He sees us, we are wrapped in righteousness and more beautiful than we can imagine. His work becomes our new life and in that, we show the beauty of a God who forgives and wraps us in a beauty that is only possible by His hand.

"If you are in Christ, when He sees you, your sins are covered—He doesn't see them. He sees you better than you see yourself."

MAX LUCADO

Where we blended in with the world before, we now stand out just as those white blooms stand out when spring arrives. What once appeared lifeless now shows not only life, but a life marked by a creative Creator. Others take note because what is now seen in our lives is something that cannot be overlooked.

Let the beauty of the Lord be on full display in your life. Live a life that causes others to take note and say, "Doggone! Look at the beauty of that life."

plant the Word—

"He made the One who did not know sin to be sin for us, so that we might become the righteousness of God in Him." (2 Corinthians 5:21, CSB)

pray the Word—

Lord, forgive me of any sin in my life. May You create a beauty in my life that captures the attention of others and brings glory to Your name. Amen.

work the Word—

Embrace the forgiveness of God. See yourself as forgiven so that you may shed the weight of what you no longer bear and shine with a beauty that speaks of God's eternal forgiveness.

DID YOU KNOW?

Legend holds that Jesus was crucified on a dogwood tree. Though the Bible does not say for certain what type of tree was used for the cross of Christ, the legend of the dogwood is interesting.

"Life moves pretty fast. If you don't stop to look around once in a while, you could miss it."

FERRIS BUELLER

MICHELLE

spring FORWARD

SPRING FORWARD—TWO WORDS I DREAD EVERY YEAR. ON THE SECOND SUNDAY IN MARCH, DAYLIGHT SAVING TIME CAUSES OUR CLOCKS TO "SPRING FORWARD" AN HOUR.

That loss of sleep hits hard, especially the first morning after the clocks have changed. You wouldn't think an hour would make such a difference, but one glance around the room at all of the yawning, zombie-like folks the day after we spring forward, and you'll know it truly does affect us.

But we can't focus on the loss of sleep; rather, we should look at how much we gain by springing forward. Daylight Saving time gives us more hours awake in the daylight to get up and experience all that God has made. The whole idea of Daylight Saving has been around for a very long time, but research shows that an Englishman named William Willett was the first big proponent for such a thing in the modern world. While out and about in town, Willett noticed that the shutters on every home were closed tightly on Spring mornings, long after the sun had risen. Meanwhile, people were using up valuable resources to make up for the lack of light in the evenings. Willett wanted people to use the free

and natural daylight that God had provided. (So if you're not a fan of Daylight Saving, Willett is the one to blame.)

We all love to "fall back" that first Sunday in November, but very few want to "spring forward" in March. Yet both are necessary to make better use of natural sunlight with Daylight Saving time. And science tells us we all need a healthy dose of sunlight. In fact, exposure to sunlight has been known to increase the brain's release of serotonin, which is a mood-boosting hormone. Also, getting into the sunlight (wearing an SPF, of course) can help your skin to create vitamin D, and vitamin D is very important to bone health and a healthy immune system. So, yay for sunlight!

You know what else we need a healthy dose of? SONlight. Yep, we need to spend time every day, basking in the presence of Jesus and soaking in His goodness, peace, and love.

Let Daylight Saving time be a reminder to enjoy the sunlight more and soak in the SONlight regularly. Now, go enjoy some of that Vitamin D!

DID YOU KNOW?
Coal conservation during World War I is what pushed governments to make Daylight Saving time a law.

plant the Word—

"Awake, my soul! Awake, harp and lyre! I will awaken the dawn." (Psalm 57:8, NIV)

pray the Word—

Lord, thank You for this beautiful world You've made, and thank You for the sunlight. Help me not to waste a single moment of today. Amen.

work the Word—

Use the opportunity of Daylight Saving time to spend an extra hour outside every day. (Of course, make sure you lather yourself in sunscreen.) Find your outside "happy place" where you can rest, think, journal, read, and pray. Maybe it's a little corner of your backyard where you've placed your favorite bench. Or maybe it's your front porch swing. Or maybe your happy place is in a nearby park. Wherever it is, go there regularly and enjoy this beautiful world. Meditate on God's goodness, and soak it all in.

shaking off
WINTER'S RUST

A TRIP SOUTH TO FLORIDA APPEARS ON OUR YEARLY CALENDAR. OUR VOYAGE HOLDS MULTIPLE PURPOSES.

For one, my wife's family lives in Florida so we can enjoy time with family.

Our second reason comes from the weather. The warmth of Florida gives us a reprieve from the still chilly temperatures at home in North Carolina.

The timing, however, stands as no coincidence. Spring Training for baseball draws us to travel across the state of Florida.

The greatest baseball players in the world practice the basic fundamentals and run through drills as they prepare for a grueling season of 162 games. As the last season ended in October, months away means a revisit to the basics, to limber up the bodies frozen by a winter's break.

Down the third base line, a set of players stretch before jogging in the outfield. A few tossed the ball off the pitcher's mound. We watched intently, then waited for the Spring Training games to begin.

"I can't wait for batting practice," I told my wife, a person who is anything but a baseball enthusiast. She endured it for me.

"Why?" she asked, still unimpressed by the events of the day.

"Because those guys can crush a ball," I quickly commented, my eyes glued to one of my favorite players.

The time finally came. A few stepped up to the plate and I moved to the edge of my seat. "Here we go. Honey, watch this! They're going to hit some missiles.

The first player dug in at the batter's box. The pitch came and he squared up to bunt the ball. It dribbled about five to six feet from the plate. Another player approached the plate and did the same thing.

"Boy, that was some missile," my wife quipped with a laugh.

Eventually, they tore the cover off the ball but first, they worked on that small fundamental that could change the game later in the season. I wanted theatrics. They needed to practice the basics. Never will I forget that Spring Training or the lesson the Lord taught me.

We often work on the big issues of our lives but neglect the small issues that need our attention.

Sometimes, the small things in life eventually lead to larger issues. An argument finds no resolution and the divide grows larger as time progresses. A little

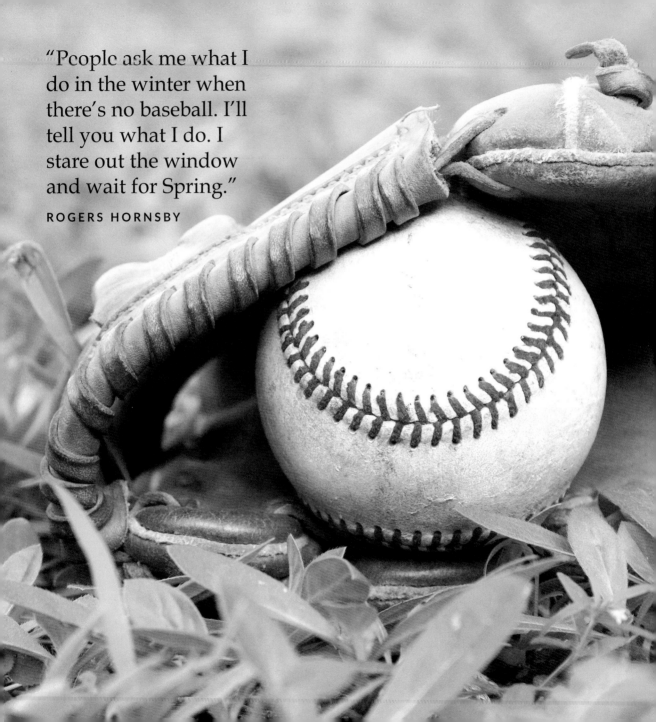

"People ask me what I do in the winter when there's no baseball. I'll tell you what I do. I stare out the window and wait for Spring."

ROGERS HORNSBY

lie snowballs into a web of lies that threatens more people. A flirty joke leads to an affair, when it could have been stopped earlier. Working on big issues matters but it's just as important to address what we perceive as smaller issues.

A verse from Song of Songs speaks to such a truth. A beautiful vineyard's produce and vibrancy stood on the cusp of destruction. The threat came not from a large predator but from the small ones. Foxes tore through the vineyard, wrecking it and preventing it from flourishing. In despair, a call went out to put a stop to that which threatened the life of a vineyard that offered so much.

A new season gives us a chance to refocus. Life changes when we look to even the smallest details in pursuit of something more. Our attention turns to the small foxes in our lives that destroy the beauty of this life. It's time to run those foxes out because our vineyard of life is coming into season.

plant the Word—

"Catch the foxes for us—the little foxes that ruin the vineyards—for our vineyards are in bloom." (Song of Songs 2:15, CSB)

pray the Word—

Dear Lord, help us to see the small sins that are damaging our lives and negatively impacting our testimony. Open our eyes to see that which has been overlooked before. We want our lives to be beautiful and vibrant, a reflection of You in all seasons.

work the Word—

The apostle Paul challenged believers to examine their lives. The same instructions extend to us. The ones who search inside for signs of unrighteousness see what needs to be changed. We, then, can run those little foxes out of our lives!

DID YOU KNOW?

One of the earliest evidences of Spring Training in baseball dates back to 1870. The practices were in New Orleans and the Cincinnati Red Stockings and the Chicago White Stockings took part.

"Hope is being able to see that there is light despite all of the darkness."

DESMOND TUTU

MICHELLE

hope &
HITTERS

IN OUR HOUSE, SPRING IS OTHERWISE KNOWN AS CUBBIES SPRING TRAINING. IF YOU'RE ALSO A FAN OF THE CHICAGO CUBS, YOU KNOW THE ENTHUSIASM SURROUNDING SPRING TRAINING.

Every year, we get excited for the start of baseball season, hoping our Cubbies will be the team we know they can be and play the kind of baseball we believe they can play. And every year, they almost always break our hearts. Still, we continue to be hopeful every March, positive that this could be our year.

Because in 2016, it was! It may seem silly to everyone who isn't a Cubs fan, but when they finally won the World Series that year—after 108 years of waiting—I sobbed. I was so overcome with emotion that I could barely stand. It was a great moment. It was the victory my mom and dad didn't live to see, but I was sure they were celebrating their Cubbies in Heaven.

It was truly one of those special sports moments I'll never forget. I can live on that 2016 season and World Series win for years to come . . . but I'd sure like to have another World Series Championship to celebrate before I die.

So, each year, I approach baseball season with renewed hope, no matter how badly the Cubbies fared the season before. I always believe for the best. Some call that optimism. In Christianity, we call that faith.

Hebrews 11:1, ESV, says, "Now faith is the assurance of things hoped for, the conviction of things not seen." As Christians, we can believe for the best, knowing that God has a good plan for us (Jeremiah 29:11), and that He is a God of miracles. So, no matter how badly our lives might presently look, we can rest in Him and remain peaceful in our hearts because we know that God is in control of all. We can have hope for tomorrow.

C. S. Lewis once said that a Christian's hope isn't wishful thinking, but rather something a believer is supposed to do.

It's part of our Christian DNA. You see, even if our present circumstances are dismal, we have hope in eternal life with Jesus, which means we can go through even the toughest of days with renewed strength and supernatural joy.

Maybe you're tired of feeling like you never win. You work hard and play fair, but someone who steps on others gets to the top faster. You accomplish something you're really proud of, but someone else takes the credit. You fight for an important cause, but the culture around you mocks it. Don't give up your hope! God will win in the end, and if you are on His team, you will enjoy the eternal reward. And that's even better than a World Series!

Having hope is not in vain. In fact, you should be excited for what's to come in this life and the next!

God has a good plan! (And while you're at it, join me in cheering on the Cubbies—maybe we'll get another championship!)

plant the Word—

"But if we hope for what we do not yet have, we wait for it patiently." (Romans 8:25, NIV)

pray the Word—

Lord, I am so grateful for my life, but sometimes it's hard to see past the difficulties I face daily. Please give me hope to go on, both for this life and the next. Amen.

work the Word—

Take a few moments and reflect on a time when you were struggling, and it felt like you were in a losing season. Then, reflect on a time when everything seemed to fall into place, and you enjoyed a winning streak. Were you able to find hope amidst each of these seasons? If not, how can you do things differently next time so you can hold onto your hope?

the cloud
OF GREEN

THE FLOWERS BLOOM. THE TREES EXPLODE WITH THE SIGNS OF NEW LIFE. WHAT COMES WITH THE BEAUTY IS A CLOUD OF GREEN THAT HOVERS OVER MANY AREAS IN OUR COUNTRY.

Pollen. A six-letter curse word to so many who suffer from allergies. As winter featured accessories of toboggans, coats, mittens, and scarfs, a new season presents alterations to the accessories. As spring comes, we carry tissues and allergy tablets, fighting off the invasion of that which disrupts our health.

Pollen covers the car, turning any vehicle to a shade of greenish yellow regardless of the original paint scheme. Front and back porches develop a dusting reminiscent of the winter's snow but a variant in color and reaction to those who see it. Airborne particles eventually land only to be launched skyward by a lawnmower working its way through the yard. Wash the car on Monday. Pollen covers it on Tuesday.

People capture pictures of the green tint outside their windows, an abundance of particles sweeping the area in such a way a camera shows the cloud of pollen. Some of the images look as if they were Hollywood produced, an over-the-top work of a graphic artist to heighten the effect. These images are no work of fiction. The presence of the particles shows in the eyes of a friend, the sneezing of a stranger, and in the line at the local pharmacy.

Every season of life presents its upside as well as its downside. For the beauty of the blooms, we battle the pollen. We escape to the outdoors even if it means a little sneezing and congestion might result.

Though it returns, a little rain offers a temporary cleansing. But through it all, what are we focused on more—the beauty or the struggle?

The same question rises for our lives in general. Are we captivated by the beauty of this life, or do we live in frustration of the struggles? When Paul wrote to the Corinthians, he sought to refocus them by encouraging them. The Corinthian believers lived in a place of rampant evil. Just as we know struggle, the Corinthians experienced struggle. Paul encouraged them with a hope for all seasons, hoping to offset any discouragement they endured.

Paul's concern showed as he pointed out the temporary nature of the afflictions of life. What might be bad is nothing in comparison to the beauty that is coming. Though the pollen seems thick, the radiance of new life means better is on the way. There is pain but it lasts for a moment. What God is doing lasts for eternity.

What's your focus? Do you focus on the little annoyances of this life or look beyond it to see the vast beauty of what is all around you? Don't

"I am convinced that life is 10 percent what happens to me and 90 percent of how I react to it. And so it is with you . . . we are in charge of our attitudes."

CHUCK SWINDOLL

let affliction (temporary) overtake the outlook (extended). Open your eyes today to see beyond the bad as you discover all that is good.

plant the Word—

"For our momentary light affliction is producing for us an absolutely incomparable eternal weight of glory. So we do not focus on what is seen, but what is unseen. For what is seen is temporary, but what is unseen is eternal." (2 Corinthians 4:17-18, CSB)

pray the Word—

Lord, we want an attitude that is pleasing to You, one that exudes thankfulness rather than constant grumbling. Open our eyes to see the beauty before us and when there are afflictions, help us to maintain our joy throughout.

work the Word—

Pay attention today and every day. Are we complaining more often than we are praising? When Satan throws something for us to complain about, let's turn around and find two reasons to praise God in that moment. Life presents struggles, but those are temporary. The gifts of God are eternal, worthy of our praise all day.

DID YOU KNOW?

According to the Asthma and Allergy Foundation of America, the worst place to live in the United States for those with seasonal allergies is Scranton, Pennsylvania. Richmond, Virginia ranks as second.

"The key is not the 'will
to win' . . . everybody has
that. It is the will to prepare
to win that is important."

LEGENDARY COACH BOB KNIGHT

MICHELLE

march
MADNESS

AS A FORMER SPORTSWRITER, DIEHARD INDIANA HOOSIERS BASKETBALL FAN, AND LIFELONG CHEERLEADER, I PRETTY MUCH LIVE FOR MARCH MADNESS.

It's one of my favorite parts of Spring! The minute the pairings are announced, thousands of basketball lovers start filling in their brackets, in hopes of predicting who will win the National Championship. While we're doing that, coaching staffs all over the United States are putting together game tape of their upcoming opponent. They are in total preparation mode, trying to figure out their opponent's weaknesses, strengths, go-to plays, as well as individual player's strengths, weaknesses, and patterns. The head coach studies the other team's game footage to notice the screens, the cuts, the movement before the shot, as well as how the team gets its best players into position to make the key plays.

Why? To gain an advantage in the upcoming faceoff. Because if you know what to expect from your opponent, you'll be better prepared to outmaneuver him and come away with a win.

Guess what? That same strategy applies when dealing with the enemy in our spiritual lives. It's good to know details about our enemy—the devil—so that we can be aware of his tricks and trademark moves. We know from the Word of God that Satan is the father of all lies. Knowing that, when he comes to you and whispers in your ear, "You're not worthy; you'll never succeed in life; God doesn't care about you," you can say, "Those things aren't true because they are coming from the father of all lies. In fact, if Satan is telling me those things, the exact opposite must be true: I am worthy! I will succeed in life! God does care about me!"

Conversely, you need to be aware that the devil is also studying you and watching your "game film." He sees what play worked on you in the past, and he will run it over and over again to try and trip you up and stop your victory.

If he knows you're a worrier, he will give you lots of things to worry about until you take the bait. So, don't fall for his tricks. Just like in basketball, we must keep our guard up in our spiritual lives. We have to stay in the Word of God. We have to spend time in prayer. And we need to take time each day to meditate on the scriptures that pertain to whatever battle we happen to be fighting at that particular time in our lives.

For example, if you're in the middle of a financial crisis right now, you should be reading and confessing scriptures about your Heavenly Father being your provider. Say: "My Father owns the cattle on a thousand hills, according to Psalms 50:10, and He will provide for me!" Speak: "According to John

10:10, my God has come that I might have life and have it more abundantly."

Furthermore, in order to defeat the enemy, we should put on the full armor of God every single day (Ephesians 6:10-18). Think of it as your mandatory uniform. Just like a basketball player needs his team uniform, his socks, and his basketball shoes; you need every single piece of the armor of God to be prepared for battle.

Here's the best news. Though these basketball teams heading into the NCAA tourney have no idea if they will win that next game, we have a different situation. See, no matter how much they prepare and practice, somebody still has to lose. There can only be one national champion. But, as Christians, we are guaranteed a win in the game of life. First Corinthians 15:57, ESV, says, "But thanks be to God, who gives us the victory through our Lord Jesus Christ."

Now, that doesn't mean our opponent is going to throw in the towel and give up. He will still try to aggravate us every chance he gets, but we will still win! You're a winner, so live with victory in your heart and mind today!

P.S. Go Hoosiers!

plant the Word—

"Keep a cool head. Stay alert. The Devil is poised to pounce, and would like nothing better than to catch you napping. Keep your guard up." (1 Peter 5:8, MSG)

pray the Word—

Help me to be vigilant, God, and prepared to fight the good fight of faith, and thank You for going through every battle with me. Amen.

work the Word—

Grab your journal and list the challenges you're facing today. Now, find at least two scriptures you can stand on pertaining to each battle.

DID YOU KNOW?

March Madness began with eight teams playing against each other in 1939, where Oregon beat Ohio State to claim that first tournament title.

ANDY

reminders of OLD DANGERS

THOUGH BREATH-TAKING TO LOOK AT, THEY SERVE AS REMINDERS OF DANGERS PAST. THOSE DANGERS INEVITABLY RETURN WITH THE SEASON.

Though winter drove the residents away, the Spring promises they will return and will occupy a new area.

My friend sent me a picture from her walk in the early Spring.

"Check this out," she texted as she attached a picture she snapped in her backyard.

I curiously looked at the photo. From the first sight, it looked like a honeycomb for bees, at least it did to me. "Cool pic. What is that?" I texted back, pretty sure I was wrong about my initial thoughts about what she captured.

"It's a hornet's nest around back. This is what the remnants look like after the winter strips away the outside covering."

The picture was breath-taking. Her love of Spring and gift of photography meshed to give me an idea.

Though it looked beautiful, it served as a reminder of where danger lurked earlier. It also served as a reminder that the danger would come again, but typically in a new location.

Every season in nature presents dangers, just as every season of life features danger. The remnants of a hornet's nest send the message to keep our eyes and ears open. Those who fail to pay attention can feel the wrath of the very hornets that once called that place home.

I stared at the picture—something that hung beautifully and was masterfully designed actually held a deathtrap to those allergic and, at minimum, a great deal of pain to those stung by what was housed within.

From that moment, I began searching for the signs of danger around our house. Would the hornets return to the same area? Usually they move a little, but sometimes, they build on to what was before. Would a new swarm take up residence in our woods?

Sin leaves its mark on our lives. Though completely forgiven by Jesus, there are scars of what was. Paul consistently reflected on that former life of his and how the Lord delivered him into new life.

He shared so many warnings in his letters to individuals and churches, cautioning them to avoid the dangers this world presents. Paul identified the fruit of the Spirit and the work of the flesh in Galatians 5. Romans 8 tells us that the danger of a fleshly mindset leads to death.

"We must learn by experience to avoid either trains of thought or social situations which for us (not necessarily for everyone) lead to temptations. Like motoring—don't wait till the last minute before you put on the brakes but put them on, gently and quietly, while the danger is still a good way off."

C. S. LEWIS

The Thessalonica believers received a short but absolute direction. Paul said that they should get as far away from any time of evil as possible. His instruction was to keep their eyes open and maintain a safe distance. See the signs of dangers. Recognize them. Don't poke the hornet's nest of sin as it will leave a mark.

Around us each day are the signs of sin and danger. Be aware as they are around every corner. As the exterior is peeled away, we can see what is housed within, that which we want no part of in life.

Pay attention today and every day. Are we complaining more often than we are praising? When Satan throws something for us to complain about, let's turn around and find two reasons to praise God in that moment. Life presents struggles, but those are temporary. The gifts of God are eternal, worthy of our praise all day.

plant the Word—

"Stay away from every kind of evil." (1 Thessalonians 5:18, CSB)

pray the Word—

Dear Lord, reveal to us the dangers that exist in this world, that which can harm us spiritually and physically. Help us remain aware in all seasons of life and keep us drawn to that which leads to life. Strengthen us to stay away, to stand strong, and walk closely with You.

work the Word—

What dangers exist around you today? Some are clearly identifiable while others are overlooked. Keep your eyes wide open to see the warning signals of dangers present and dangers to come. Those who live with eyes wide open typically avoid the traps that others struggle to avoid and escape.

DID YOU KNOW?

The Asian giant hornet, nicknamed "murder hornet," is the deadliest hornet in the world. The female worker hornet can grow to lengths of an inch and a half. Though they pose the greatest threat to honeybees, the hornet can kill humans as it packs immense amounts of venom.

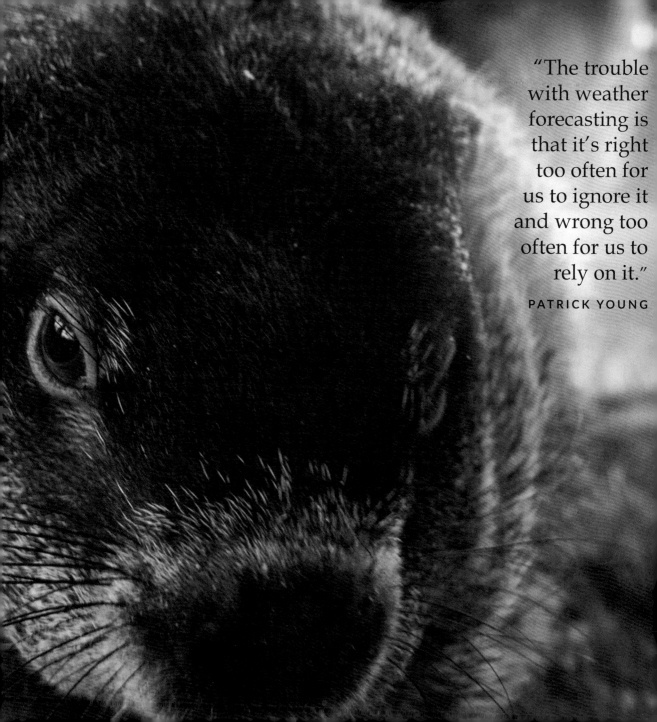

"The trouble with weather forecasting is that it's right too often for us to ignore it and wrong too often for us to rely on it."

PATRICK YOUNG

MICHELLE

celebrating
GROUNDHOG DAY

AH, GROUNDHOG DAY. A DAY THAT MANY OF US DON'T ACTIVELY MARK DOWN ON OUR CALENDARS—BUT NONETHELESS, WE'RE STILL CURIOUS ABOUT PUNXSUTAWNEY PHIL'S PREDICTION EACH YEAR.

Legend says, of course, that if the famous groundhog sees his shadow and crawls back into his den, there will be six more weeks of winter. But if he doesn't see his shadow, then there will be an early Spring. Like most people, I'm always hoping for the latter.

However, many folks don't put much stock in Phil's predictions. In fact, his forecasts have only been accurate about 39 percent of the time. Still, it is so depressing when it's announced that Phil saw his shadow and projected another six weeks of winter. That happened last year, and when I heard the news, I immediately said out loud, "Stupid groundhog."

On those days when we receive bad news, or it seems like the dark days of winter will never end, isn't it comforting to know we have the promise of something way better that has nothing to do with a groundhog? We have the promise of Jesus and an eternity with Him in Heaven. Those promises are found in His Holy Word, the Bible. He has given us descriptions of just how wonderful life will be in Heaven, where there are bountiful blessings and no more sorrow. And He has promised that, if we confess our sins and believe that Jesus is the Son of God and give our lives to Him, we will spend eternity in Heaven with Him.

While Phil's predictions are completely mythical and unreliable, God's Word and His promises are true prophecies of the future.

Many Bible scholars agree that most of God's prophecies in the Bible have already been fulfilled. You can count on this future one to come true, too. We don't need to be concerned with the groundhog's shadow. After all, as Christians, we are living in the shadow of the cross. Now that's worth celebrating!

DID YOU KNOW?

Punxsutawney Phil's official name is Punxsutawney Phil, Seer of Seers, Sage of Sages, Prognosticator of Prognosticators, and Weather Prophet Extraordinary.

plant the Word—

"But to all who believed him and accepted him, he gave the right to become children of God." (John 1:12, NLT)

pray the Word—

Lord, I thank You for Your promise of Heaven. Whatever happens today, help me keep my eyes on Your promises and my relationship with You. I love You, Jesus. Amen.

work the Word—

Look up Punxsutawney Phil's prediction for Spring this year. Over the next few weeks, assess the accuracy of his prediction in your journal. Now, look up some of God's promises and the prophesies He told to His prophets. How accurate have those "forecasts" been?

As you do this exercise, it's important to understand there are two kinds of prophecies—predictive and forthtelling. A predictive prophecy predicts what will happen. A forthtelling prophecy is when God speaks concerning this present hour. So when you study the Bible to see how many prophecies have already been fulfilled, you are looking for predictive prophecies.

"Never lose an opportunity of seeing anything beautiful, for beauty is God's handwriting."

RALPH WALDO EMERSON

ANDY

a longer DAY

THROUGHOUT MOST OF THE NATION, THE CLOCK JUMPS FORWARD AN HOUR JUST BEFORE SPRING ARRIVES. EACH YEAR, WE STRUGGLE TO RECLAIM THE LOST HOUR OF SLEEP INITIALLY, BUT A GREAT BLESSING.

Winter's grip loosens.

Daylight extends further into the evening.

When the day of work ends, light remains, offering opportunities for family activities. Occasionally, it's a night of miniature golf, but one of the simple, frequent excursions is a simple walk around our neighborhood.

"Daddy, can we go for a walk after supper?" one of my daughters will ask on a given night during Spring. They alternate who asks and often say that it is the other sister who wants to know.

"Sure, if it's okay with your mother," I normally respond, knowing that my wife is always up for a walk.

The girls ride their scooters. Brady, my son, gets in the stroller. Crystal and I walk and talk. Laughter fills the air as the sound of shoes and wheels raking gravel speaks to a new season's arrival. A half-hour flies by as the world is set aside for time together as we squeeze out the last few minutes of daylight. Winter closed the days out early but Spring extends the possibility of what a day can offer.

We've been given a little extra time. We refuse to waste the blessing.

Daylight calls out to the soul inside. A ray of sunshine lights the way for a family moment. We bask in the light, taking in each second, until the sun descends in the west and gives way to nightfall.

Our venture brings us the joy of seeing the blooms on bushes and trees. An unexpected squirrel darts across the road, much to the joy of our young children. They ask questions about a range of topics and occasionally, we flee from local guinea hens that draw a little too close.

Memories come from those early evening Spring strolls down the road. Our bodies benefit from the exercise while our minds embrace the respite from the demands of life. Thirty minutes escape quickly but the quality of the time far outweighs the quantity.

Psalm 90 features a call out to God for understanding. The words ask the Lord to teach us to number our days. The reasoning—to develop wisdom in our lives.

The assumption of eighty years on Earth fools many to waste days in their lives. The erroneous thought that there will always be tomorrow leads to wasted opportunities. Spring offers a little more light, an extra few moments to enjoy what God has given to us.

Have we developed the wisdom in our hearts to understand that these moments are fleeting? Do we understand that tomorrow is not guaranteed?

Let's pray each day that the Lord gives us wisdom in understanding the brevity of this life. Let's ask Him to open our eyes to the opportunities to enjoy what He's given us.

plant the Word—

"Teach us to number our days carefully so that we may develop wisdom in our hearts." (Psalm 90:12, CSB)

pray the Word—

Heavenly Father, remind us each day that the moment we have is all that we are guaranteed on this earth. Teach us to embrace the day and the opportunity You place before us.

work the Word—

With added daylight, what can you do today to make a memory? The longer day offers us a chance to enjoy life outdoors a little longer.

DID YOU KNOW?

The Department of Health and Human Services recommends at least 150 minutes of moderate aerobic exercise per week. A thirty-minute walk each day will help you exceed the baseline numbers and greatly benefit your life.

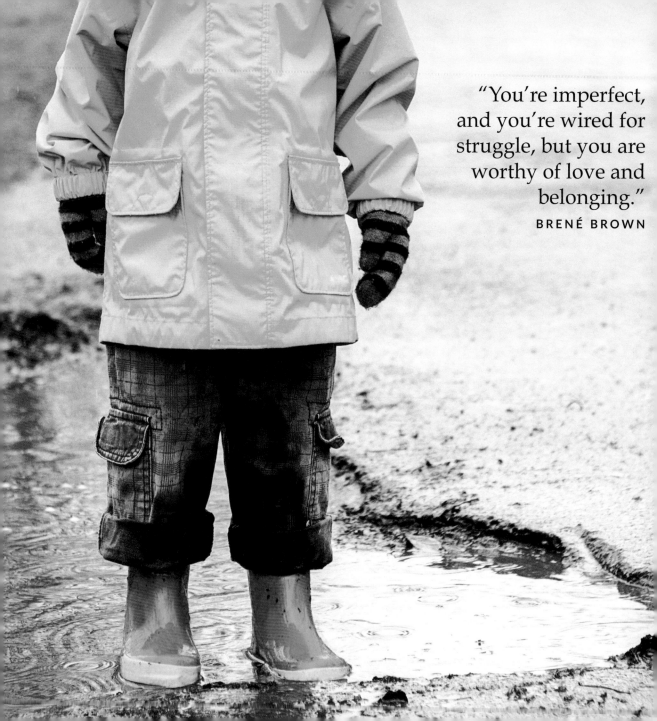

"You're imperfect, and you're wired for struggle, but you are worthy of love and belonging."
BRENÉ BROWN

MICHELLE

pothole
PROBLEMS

EVER SEE THAT OLD GEICO COMMERCIAL ABOUT POTHOLES? A CUTE LITTLE SPORTS CAR HITS A BIG OLE POTHOLE IN THE ROAD, CAUSING A FLAT TIRE AND LOTS OF AGGRAVATION FOR THE DRIVER.

Then the pothole says in a sweet Southern accent, "Oh no! Your tire's all flat and junk. Did I do that? Here let me get my cellular out and call you a wrecker. Oh shoot! I got no phone cuz I'm just a pothole . . . so . . . 'K bye!"

Sure, that commercial is pretty funny, but driving over a pothole isn't. Every spring in Indiana, when the snow melts, and the roads are once again visible, you can see the brand-new batch of bumps, holes, and potholes—some big enough to fall in!

I think those potholes can be a lot like our own imperfections of the heart. You can only hide them for so long. Eventually, the people in your life will see "the real you," and you'll be forced to deal with those holes in your heart. You might even try to hide them from God, but guess what? He knows about every single one . . . and He still loves you.

Just like the potholes in the snow-covered pavement, our imperfections grow deeper and wider when we try to hide them. But once you reveal those imperfections to God, He can fix them. What's revealed can be healed. It's the same way with the potholes in the pavement.

While they are hidden away under the snow, the road crews can't even find them in order to fill and fix them. But once the warmer temperatures of spring melt the snow, those once-hidden potholes are exposed and can finally be repaired, making the road as good as new.

Be honest. Have you been covering up the imperfections of your heart? Do you have sin you've been hiding that you need to give to God today?

He already knows about all of our imperfections anyway, so go ahead and confess those things to your Heavenly Father and ask Him to fill up those potholes with His unconditional love, all-encompassing forgiveness, and supernatural peace.

DID YOU KNOW?

There are reportedly about fifty-five million potholes in the United States.

work the Word—

Revealing your sin to God takes a lot of courage. But often, it's even harder to be honest with ourselves. If you feel like you're stuck in a deep, dark pothole because you can't face what you've done or forgive yourself, now is the time to shake off that guilt and condemnation and crawl out of that hole.

Even if you're disappointed in yourself. Even if you let your family down in some way. Even if you have been away from the Lord. God still loves you. God is a God of grace, and He is ready and willing to forgive you, but you have to forgive yourself. God doesn't expect perfection. If He did, He wouldn't have used Peter in the Bible because he certainly wasn't perfect. I mean, he cut off a guy's ear! Remember that story?

When they came to arrest Jesus in the Garden of Gethsemane, Peter cut off the guard's right ear. He is also the one who told Jesus, "Hey these other disciples may forsake you, but I never will," and then he denied knowing Jesus three times before twenty-four hours had passed. Peter was so distraught, the Word says, "After thinking about what he'd done, he wept."

But how did that story end? After the resurrection, Jesus went to find Peter. Jesus pursued Peter and gave him another chance. Guess what? The Lord is pursuing you today! He wants to give you another chance, but you have to allow Him to do that, and you have to forgive yourself. There's freedom in forgiveness. Don't you want to get free today?

plant the Word—

"Whoever conceals their sins does not prosper, but the one who confesses and renounces them finds mercy." (Proverbs 28:13, NIV)

pray the Word—

Lord, I ask You to forgive my sins and make me new. Smooth out my flaws and fill me with Your love and peace. Thank You, God, for forgiving me and loving me no matter what. Guide me on the path You have mapped out for my life. I love You. Amen.

ANDY

time
TO BUILD

WE ALL NEED A PLACE TO STAY, A PLACE TO CALL HOME. JUST AS WE ENSURE A PLACE FOR OURSELVES, WE CHECK ITS STRENGTH AND STABILITY AS IT HOUSES OUR CHILDREN.

Spring brings an abundance of activities. The birds meticulously build a place to call home. Each nest is comprised of different materials, its construction a work of beauty.

The winged animals choose a location. Some choose a place covered from the elements, under the covering of a front porch of a home or a church. Others select an area of branches in a tree, the distance between branches not too wide to hold the construction.

A stick at a time, they construct a home. Eggs will eventually lay inside so the nest must cradle securely, keeping the eggs from tumbling to the ground. Storms will come. The pouring rains of spring and summer will wash out much of what lays on the ground, so the height keeps the nest from washing away. Its strength ensures it will not collapse even when the hardest rains pour.

Finally, the birds stabilize their nests so strong winds pose less threats. Winds blow but a secure nest keeps in place when a breeze turns into a bluster. The best of the nest endure the year, the remnants seen later.

A walk in the woods draws our eyes to see where the birds' construction took place. We point out the ones we find, making sure our girls see the nests for themselves.

The Bible teaches us to build our foundation in a solid place. Every life has a foundation but not every life is constructed in a way to stand throughout the course of time. Storms of life will strike at some point. Winds intensify, rains pour down, and waves crash in such a way that the foundation of life is tested.

Blueprints for biblical living sit inside the Bible. Jesus warned at the end of the Sermon on the Mount to check our foundation. Paul gave insight on how to build wisely as well. Paul implored that Christ is the cornerstone. As He is the cornerstone of our lives, we are constructed on the immovable rock.

Paul also said that life needs to stand on the work of the Prophets and the apostles. That work is the Bible, using the wisdom of the Word to stand upon at all times, a foundation that never shifts or wavers. Finally, Paul recognized God as the Ultimate Builder.

The birds take every measure to make sure their home stands. Their lives, as well as the lives of their eggs, needs stability to weather the storm. Maybe we can learn something from the birds. It may just be

"Make it your goal to build strong foundations for your life — foundations constructed from prayer and the truths of God's Word."

BILLY GRAHAM

HOLY BIBLE

that we need to rebuild our lives this spring, to do so as the Bible instructs, because storms will come, and we want a life that is built to last.

plant the Word—

"So then you are no longer foreigners and strangers, but fellow citizens with the saints, and members of God's household, built on the foundation of the apostles and prophets, with Christ Jesus Himself as the cornerstone." (Ephesians 2:19-20, CSB)

pray the Word—

Dear Lord, help us to build our lives in a way that will stand even when storms arise. By Your plan and by Your hand construct our lives for us. We need You to help us have a solid foundation.

work the Word—

Build your life on Jesus. Just as a homebuilder focuses on every detail of the home, let's use God's Word to build up every area of our lives. He has proven to be strong enough and those truly built on Him will not be shaken.

DID YOU KNOW?

Bald eagles are known to construct some of the most well-built nests. These habitations are used year after year and are known for size and strength. One such nest discovered had a depth of twenty feet and a weight of two tons.

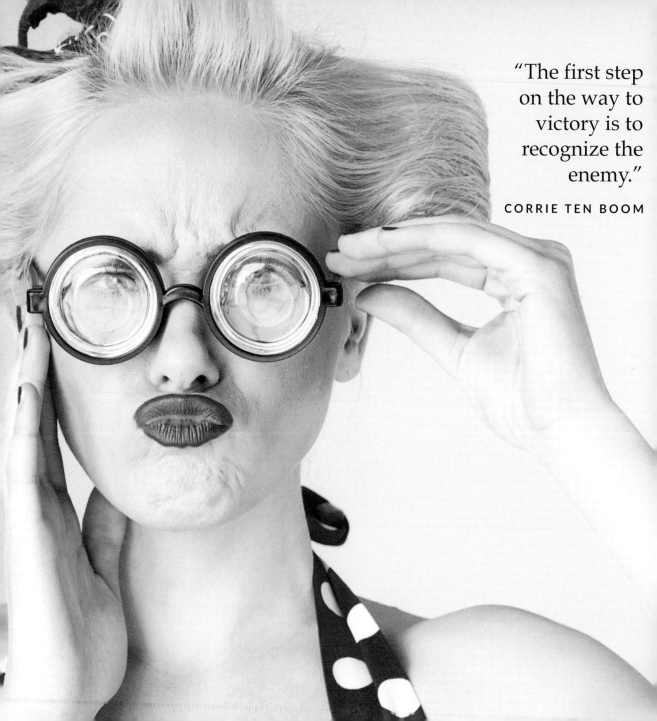

"The first step
on the way to
victory is to
recognize the
enemy."

CORRIE TEN BOOM

MICHELLE

i didn't see
THAT COMING

I DON'T ALWAYS KNOW THE ACTUAL DATE. I KNOW THE DAY OF THE WEEK, AND I AM AWARE OF WHAT I NEED TO DO ON ANY GIVEN DAY, BUT THERE ARE TIMES WHEN THE ACTUAL DATE GETS BY ME. ONE DAY OF THE YEAR, THAT OVERSIGHT SERVES AS MY DOWNFALL.

I've never paid much attention to April Fool's Day. I know it's on the calendar, and I understand the tradition, but most of the time, that day just isn't on my radar. While I've never thought of myself as being the super gullible type, every year on April Fool's Day, I am drawn into the craziest of scenarios, falling for outrageous tales hook, line, and sinker.

One year, my friend from across the miles convinced me I'd been chosen as part of a new reality TV series about working writers. It wasn't until I started sharing the news with my husband that I realized I'd been duped. Another year, a colleague called with news that we'd won an all-expense paid vacay to Ireland as part of an Ancestry DNA promotion, and I excitedly started digging into my mother's Irish family tree before laughter ensued on the other end of the cellphone. Another year, I read something on Facebook about a Chick-fil-A opening in our little town, and I was already dreaming of those amazing chicken nuggets when my sister informed me it was an April Fool's Day hoax. #nonuggetsforme

Why do I allow this to happen? As if a carbon copy of the previous year, I forget the date and I am fooled once again.

The trouble is that my guard isn't up. Because I don't play tricks or tell outlandish stories on the first day of April, I forget that others do. Instead of thinking about what could happen on that day, I treat it as just another day, believing everything everyone tells me until someone gets me good.

The more I think about it, the more I realize this is a good lesson for us all. Our guard must be up, at all times, and in all seasons. The devil has a way of telling lies that is quite convincing, and he doesn't reserve his trickery to just one day a year. In fact, Jesus refers to him as the father of lies. Or as my mama would describe him, "liar, liar, pants on fire."

From the beginning of time, the enemy has distorted, lied, and deceived people, especially targeting those who do not have their guard up.

Think about it--he drew in Eve with a lie, didn't he? He even tried to deceive and tempt Jesus into sin, although that one didn't work out so well for the enemy. Throughout Scripture, we identify the devil's main strategy and strength—the power to deceive.

But here's the good news: We have the weapons to stand up against him and his lies. Through the wisdom of God, through His Word, and through the presence of the Holy Spirit in our lives, we can recognize and defend against every deception. We just need to be ready, spiritual guns blazing.

Every day, before our feet hit the floor, we need to be battle ready. Simply pray, "Lord, I commit myself and this day to You. Help me to hear Your voice above all of the chaos and help me to grow in discernment. Protect me, Lord, and help me to recognize the enemy's lies and tactics. Amen." With God, we can identify the enemy's deception and not be labeled a fool on any day of the year.

plant the Word—

"You are of your father the devil, and your will is to do your father's desires. He was a murderer from the beginning, and has nothing to do with the truth, because there is no truth in him. When he lies, he speaks out of his own character, for he is a liar and the father of lies." (1 Peter 5:8, NLT)

pray the Word—

Heavenly Father, prepare me for what the day may bring. Expose the deception of the enemy and help me to see through his lies. Lord, give me the wisdom I need to stand each day. I love You, Amen.

work the Word—

Follow the advice of Paul in Ephesians 6 to prepare for the day. Start with reading some Scripture and pray that God opens your spiritual eyes. Weigh everything you hear against the Word of God—does it align with what God says or is it contradictory to the Word of God?

DID YOU KNOW?

On April 1, 1996, Taco Bell duped people, announcing it had agreed to buy Philadelphia's Liberty Bell and planned to rename it the "Taco Liberty Bell."

take a swing
THIS SPRING

PRACTICE MARKED THE OTHER SEASONS OF THE YEAR. EARLY MORNING TENNIS PRACTICE HELPED US BEAT THE HEAT OF THE DAY DURING THE SUMMER. AS AUTUMN ARRIVED, WE PRACTICED A LITTLE LONGER AS THE TEMPERATURES COOLED, AND IN THE WINTER, WARMUPS NEVER CAME OFF AS WE SQUEEZED IN EVERY CHANCE WE HAD TO GET BETTER.

Spring offered the payoff for the practice. The regular season began, and we traveled to play on campuses in our area.

As my senior season began in high school, I tried to appreciate the moment. Coach Biles fought for me in that semester, so I decided I'd run through a wall for him.

A date loomed late in the season. We faced Walter Williams High School and Coach delivered one of his best speeches.

"I don't think Southern has ever beaten Williams . . . but we can be the first," he assured as he prepared us for the match.

His belief in us made us believe the impossible was actually possible.

As the match progressed, one of our players won their match. That was one point. Another match ended with another Southern victory, and we began to believe.

By the end of the day, the giant fell. We defeated the crosstown Goliath, a Spring day we will never forget. Twenty-five years later, Coach Biles and I sat down for lunch together and the moment arose in our conversation.

"What a special day," I commented.

"Yes, it was. That was a huge victory for the program," Coach said, his signature smile a flashback to that day in Burlington two and a half decades earlier.

This season offers us a chance to step up and slay the giants that stand before us. The prior seasons prepared us for the moment we face right now.

We have a coach, Jesus, who stands ready to guide us and to help us overcome. This is our season to take a swing and topple what seemed impossible to overcome before. Do we have the courage to step up and take down that giant today?

David stood up when everyone else cowered in the distance. The shepherd boy and eventual king recognized how God prepared him for the showdown. He stepped up when no one else would. Saul tried to stop him, but David pointed out two things. First, he pointed to God's preparation. The beasts of the field posed great threats, but God enabled him to prevail.

"Instead of telling God about the big mountain in front of us, let's tell the mountains about our big God."

KRISTEN WELCH

Second, he pointed out God's presence by saying that it was God who would deliver him.

Don't let this season be a missed opportunity. What previous seasons and situations instilled in you gives you what you need to push forward and overcome now. Also, the presence of humanity's greatest support is with you—His name is Jesus! Take a swing and decades later, you will look back and praise Him for it.

plant the Word—

"David put his hand in the bag, took out a stone, slung it, and hit the Philistine on his forehead. The stone sank into his forehead, and he fell on his face to the ground." (1 Samuel 17:49, CSB)

pray the Word—

Dear Heavenly Father, give us courage. Push us to step up and take a shot today. Rather than cower in fear as giants taunt, help us to rise up in faith today. When victory comes, remind us that You deserve the glory and praise.

work the Word—

Take some time to go through the Bible and list the times the Lord did the impossible. Notice how the Lord took ordinary people and accomplished extraordinary things through them. Look at people like Moses, David, Peter, Paul, and so many more, then see the champion that God has created in you.

DID YOU KNOW?

Helen Keller became the first person with deafblindness to earn a Bachelor of Arts degree. Her giants were not as big as her drive for life.

"Patience is not the ability to wait but the ability to keep a good attitude while waiting."

JOYCE MEYER

MICHELLE

perfect TIMING

IF YOU'RE ANYTHING LIKE ME, YOU PROBABLY CAN'T WAIT TO PLANT YOUR SPRINGTIME FLOWERS AND ENJOY THEIR COLORFUL BLOOMS. ON THAT FIRST DAY OF WARM SPRINGTIME WEATHER EACH YEAR, I'M READY TO PUT ON MY LEOPARD CROCS, SLIP ON MY GARDENING GLOVES, AND PLANT THE FLOWERS I'VE ALREADY PURCHASED THAT HAVE BEEN WAITING IN MY GARAGE UNTIL THE WEATHER TURNED WARM ENOUGH FOR PLANTING. JUST AS I'M ABOUT TO GET ALL "DIGGY" WITH IT, MY HUSBAND SAYS, "IT'S TOO EARLY TO PLANT FLOWERS. . . . IF YOU PLANT THEM NOW, YOU'LL BE SORRY." I TRY TO IGNORE HIM, BUT HE CONTINUES, "I'M TELLING YOU; IT'S TOO EARLY. IT MAY BE WARM TODAY, BUT YOU CAN HAVE A HARD FROST IN INDIANA ALL THE WAY UP TO THE MIDDLE OF MAY. I ONCE FISHED A TOURNAMENT IN MAY, AND WE HAD SLEET."

He says it every year. I know he could be right, but the urge to plant those big, beautiful begonias is too strong, so I plant them anyway. And I've had to cover those plants with plastic several years due to freezing temps. Some years, my flowers survived, and other years, they did not. Jeff is too kind to give me the whole, "I told you so" speech, but he was right—it was too early to plant flowers in Indiana.

This year, I listened to his advice, and even though my sister put out her flowers on that first warm day of Spring, I resisted the urge. Four days later, it snowed. SNOWED the third week of April! Boy, was I glad I hadn't put my flowers out.

Patience when planting flowers can mean the difference between vibrant, thriving flowers and shriveled, dead ones. I think the same principle of patience holds true in many areas of life. We hardly ever want to wait for the things we desire, but God often makes us wait. That's because God's timing is perfect, and He knows what the future holds. He may delay certain blessings until a better season; a season in which your blessings will thrive and multiply.

It's not always easy to wait, but we can wait in faith, knowing that God's timing is much better than our timing. He is good, and He knows far more than we do.

He doesn't want you to plant your spiritual flowers too soon. In fact, He is preparing a season in the future when you can enjoy healthy, thriving flowers. God's divine delays are always in our best interest, so listen for His voice, and follow His lead. What He has in store for you will definitely be worth the wait.

plant the Word—

"But do not forget this one thing, dear friends: With the Lord a day is like a thousand years, and a thousand years are like a day. The Lord is not slow in keeping His promise, as some understand slowness. Instead He is patient with you, not wanting anyone to perish, but everyone to come to repentance." (2 Peter 3:8-9, NIV)

pray the Word—

God, I trust You with my future. Help me to be patient and learn to wait in faith on all that You have planned for me. And help me to praise You for the divine delays. I love You. Amen.

work the Word—

Think about some things in your life that you have received after long periods of prayer. Can you see any reasons why you might not have received what you asked for immediately? Then, in your journal, write down some things you are asking God for today. In the future, you'll be able to look back on them from a different season of life, and maybe even understand God's timing in a deeper, more appreciative way.

DID YOU KNOW?
Developing patience may contribute to better mental and physical health. It's true, according to a study by Baylor Associate Professor Sarah A. Schnitker and UC Davis Professor Robert Emmons.

short sleeves by day,
SWEATSHIRT AT NIGHT

DURING THE WINTER, PANTS ARE THE ONLY OPTION, BUT WITH A CHANGE OF SEASON, A CHANGE OF ATTIRE COMES. THE WARMTH OF THE SUN MEANS FEWER LAYERS ARE NEEDED TO START THE DAY. HIGHS OF SEVENTY DEGREES ALLOW US TO WEAR SHORTS IN THE DAY.

By night, though, a dip in the temperature often leads to adding more layers. The T-shirt of earlier needs a sweatshirt for comfort. A swing of twenty degrees means we need to adapt to the change or suffer.

There are some days where we begin with long sleeves, transition to short sleeves in the afternoon, only to turn back to a hoodie once the sun goes down.

As my daughters prepared to play their first ever soccer game, we experienced the changes in a short span of time. The most obvious example came from my son, Brady, who was less than a year old.

The first game began at 9:00 a.m., meaning we had to arrive at 8:45. The excitement and the anticipation fueled me that morning, but we had to make sure Brady was comfortable. A balmy fifty-six degrees with a breeze had us shivering as we walked to the field.

"Pull up his blanket," Crystal instructed as I carried him to the field.

"It is a little cold," I responded as I wrapped his furry blanket a little tighter, thankful I was carrying him as he kept me warm too.

Between the games, I shed my sweatshirt. In an hour and a half, the weather warmed and Brady, snugly wrapped, now featured a wet head, sweating beneath the blanket that no longer seemed necessary.

By the end of the second game, his little arms were red, a slight sunburn that came on quickly.

"We'll have to bring something to keep him covered from now on," Crystal pointed out as we headed to the car.

How did it happen? In a three-hour span of time, he went from shivering to sweating to sunburnt. Thus, the life of adapting the wardrobe during the season began.

We wonder what we need to wear as the season adjusts away from the cold of winter and moves closer to the heat of summer. The weather forecasters give us some insight but even then, we have to change the garments during the day.

The Bible teaches us how we should dress every day. The articles are not hanging in the closet but are found in scripture. The armor of God never needs to be adapted or changed but must be worn every day.

"Spiritual armor
is useful only if
we put it on!"

DAVID JEREMIAH

Our clothes battle the elements, but the armor of God battles the enemy. The times change. The conditions of the battle shift, but the armor covers us regardless of what battle we may face today. It covers us from head to toe.

What are you putting on this morning? Are you truly prepared for what the day may bring?

Put on the full armor of God before you walk out the door today. Each piece covers you, protecting you throughout the day. By spending a few moments in the Word, you are prepared to walk out into this world.

plant the Word—

"Put on the full armor of God so that you can stand against the tactics of the Devil." (Ephesians 6:11, CSB)

pray the Word—

Dear Lord, help us to armor up for battle before we leave the house each day. Protect us from the enemy but also prepare us to stand up against the enemy every day. Give us the strength we need and keep us clothed in Your righteousness at all times.

work the Word—

The Word of God prepares us for battle. Just as we would not go into a physical war without the necessary equipment, we should not enter the spiritual war without the proper equipment. Know His Word. Let it be the most important thing you put on today.

DID YOU KNOW?

According to askingalot.com, the average weight of a Roman's armor and gear was about forty-four pounds. As they carried these, they additionally had a backpack with rations, which added more weight.

47

"The best part of life is not just surviving, but thriving with passion and compassion and humor and style and generosity and kindness."

MAYA ANGELOU

MICHELLE

bloom where YOU'RE PLANTED

AS I WAS TAKING A WALK THROUGH MY NEIGHBORHOOD TODAY, I SPOTTED A LITTLE PURPLE FLOWER POKING THROUGH A CRACK IN THE SIDEWALK. I THOUGHT, "SPRING HAS SPRUNG RIGHT HERE IN OUR NEIGHBORHOOD SIDEWALK."

A lot of people might consider it unsightly, an intruder in the middle of a busy walkway, but I found myself impressed with this little flower. It can't be easy to grow roots and produce a flower when you sprout in a tiny crack in the concrete!

I think I've been a lot like that flower in different times of my life. I've found myself planted in places that weren't ideal. At the time, those places felt suffocating, limiting, and less than desirable for growth. They were uncomfortable spots—certainly not my choice—yet that's where I ended up for that particular season of my life.

Yes, I wanted God to pick me up, remove me from that place, and put me somewhere better. I cried out, "God, rescue me from this place." But He didn't. His answer was "no" because He had positioned me in that place for that season for a specific reason.

Like that little purple flower, I had to grow up and trust His decision on where He had put me. I had to choose to bloom where God had planted me.

In different times of our lives, we may not be thrilled where we are planted. Maybe you're not happy with the place you live, the job you work, or the season you find yourself in right now. But just because life isn't always the way we had imagined, doesn't mean we have the right to just sit around and wait for things to get better. Instead, we can choose to be happy and bloom right where we are planted. I say "choose" because it really is a choice.

We can decide to take root in the place we are in today, commit to growing there, and eventually produce blooms. Or, we can decide to uproot before we're ready, wither, and dry up. Let's choose to bloom.

Despite your circumstances, you can take steps to learn and grow right where you are. You can find joy in the Lord even when you can't find it in your circumstances. Choose today to stop living to survive and start living to thrive. And just like that little purple flower, you'll bring beauty to your world.

DID YOU KNOW?

Some flowers can grow without any dirt, including orchids, aechmea, and some varieties of daffodils.

plant the Word—

"But blessed is the one who trusts in the LORD, whose confidence is in Him. They will be like a tree planted by the water that sends out its roots by the stream. It does not fear when heat comes; its leaves are always green. It has no worries in a year of drought and never fails to bear fruit." (Jeremiah 17:7–8, NIV)

pray the Word—

Lord, reveal to me how I can bloom where I am planted. Show me how I can grow through the challenges I'm facing. And help me, Lord, to choose joy every day. I love You, Lord. Amen.

work the Word—

Consider the areas of your life in which you feel you are only surviving rather than thriving. In your journal, create a list of ways you could grow—and maybe even blossom—in that environment.

ANDY

come on, SPRING BREAK!

THE EYES OF STUDENTS FROM MIDDLE SCHOOL TO COLLEGE SCAN CALENDARS TO SEE WHEN THEIR FAVORITE WEEK WILL COME. SPRING BREAK PROMISED SOME TIME AWAY, OPPORTUNITIES TO SLEEP LATER, A CHANCE TO TAKE A TRIP. THE JOY OF A WEEK OFF STARTED A COUNTDOWN FROM THE MOMENT CLASSES RESUMED IN JANUARY.

My senior year in high school, some of the leaders of our senior class organized a trip for Spring Break. Rather than a beach trip or time at the lake, they aligned everything so we could go on a cruise to the Bahamas.

"I'm in," I told a classmate, excited to go.

"No way I'm missing this," he assured me.

Neither of us had ever left the country. The thrill of something new had each of us longing just to get to Spring Break. And every day was one day closer.

My mom worked hard to help me afford the trip. The night before was restless in anticipation. I wanted to see. I imagined what it would look like and envisioned what I would see. When the day came, we boarded a bus and made our way south, to the port in Florida.

The size of the ship blew my mind as we boarded. Upon arrival in the islands, the beauty of the clear waters drew my attention away from everything else. I walked in the ocean and could see my toes, a completely far-fetched idea before that moment. A place of beauty told me the trip was worth the wait.

We counted the days down until that trip. Brochures could not prepare me for what I beheld in the days we spent out to sea. I still remember those moments. Of all the Spring Breaks of my life in school, that year, 1995, stands out like no other.

What are you living in anticipation of this spring? What has you excited about life and beyond this life? One of the features of 1 Thessalonians tells us about what should excite us every day. Paul wrote to the believers in Thessalonica and in every chapter, he references the coming of Christ. All five chapters point to Jesus coming!

As life happened, as persecution loomed, as struggles assailed, Paul made sure the believers knew they had something to look forward to in life and beyond. He told them to look up as what awaits is greater than anything else they could imagine.

Heaven awaits. With each passing day, His coming draws even more near than it was yesterday. Paul wrote that the words of the coming of Jesus were to serve as an encouragement.

As believers, no matter what we face, there is always something to look forward to. At some point, a trumpet will sound and Jesus will come. The brokenness of the world is left behind as we enter into a holiness and beauty our minds cannot fathom. A place of perfect peace, an atmosphere of holiness, and an eternal home awaits. Heaven is in sight. That's what we are looking forward to today.

plant the Word—

"For we say this to you by a revelation from the Lord: We who are still alive at the Lord's coming will certainly have no advantage over those who have fallen asleep. For the Lord Himself will descend from Heaven with a shout, with the archangel's voice, and with the trumpet of God, and the dead in Christ will rise first. Then we who are still alive will be caught up together with them in the clouds to meet the Lord in the air and so we will always be with the Lord." (1 Thessalonians 4:15-17, CSB)

pray the Word—

Dear Lord, what awaits us in You is far greater than anything this world offers. Keep our eyes focused on Heaven and reassure us that eternity trumps the temporary. Fill our minds with the thoughts of Heaven as we walk through this life here on Earth.

work the Word—

Though we have no images of Heaven, we do have details in the Bible about what Heaven contains. Find pictures of peaceful places on Earth and list around the picture the description of what Heaven will be like. Dig into scripture to see the depictions of Heaven and think on those descriptions each day.

DID YOU KNOW?
The reason the water is so clear in the Bahamas and other places is due to limited upwelling and is a result of the reefs surrounding those areas.

"We live under
the sun, but
our destiny is
beyond its rising
and setting!"

DAVID JEREMIAH

"The Bible will keep you from sin, or sin will keep you from the Bible."

DWIGHT L. MOODY

MICHELLE

sneaky SNAKES

EVERY FISHERMAN KNOWS THAT SPRING FISHING IS THE BEST FISHING. SO, OF COURSE, MY HUSBAND AND I COULDN'T WAIT FOR THAT FIRST SPRING MORNING WE COULD HIT THE LAKE.

After watching the sun come up, which is always beautiful on the lake, we enjoyed several hours of very productive fishing. And then, our peaceful morning was disrupted by an unwelcome visitor.

"Oh my gosh! SNAKE!" I yelled. "It's headed straight for the boat!"

My husband quickly put down his fishing rod and grabbed an oar. Even though Jeff jabbed at the water to scare off the snake so it wouldn't enter our boat, that snake kept on swimming. The closer it got, the louder I screamed! Finally, Jeff was able to discourage the creepy snake, but if he hadn't, I was ready to do whatever it took to escape—including flagging down another boat and climbing aboard the snake-free watercraft.

You see, sometimes the enemy comes at us forcefully and blatantly—just like that water snake.

When that happens, we often instinctually react the same way I did in the boat that day: screaming and doing everything possible to get away. We immediately jump into action and defend ourselves against the attack or do whatever we can to escape the enemy. But most times, the enemy comes rather sneakily. And those are the times when our guard isn't up. Those are the times when we don't see him swimming toward our boat. We're just enjoying life, fishing with our spouse, unaware that we're about to face an attack.

Maybe you've experienced this type of attack, and it's left you feeling vulnerable, exposed, and afraid. I get it. Listen, we've all been there.

That's why we have to be vigilant. We must remain aware of our surroundings and the dangers that could be lurking there, such as sin, falsities, or idols. We must be prepared for any enemy that comes at us.

The best way to do that is to keep in constant contact with God. Start each morning with prayer, asking God for guidance and protection. The Bible will serve as your map, and God will be your guide. By looking to God for direction, you will learn what to look out for and how to see the warning signs that the enemy is heading for your boat.

DID YOU KNOW?

Snakes can't chew, so they swallow their prey whole—even if it's bigger than their heads.

plant the Word—

"Devote yourselves to prayer, keeping alert in it with an attitude of thanksgiving." (Colossians 4:2, NASB)

pray the Word—

Lord, please reveal the snakes that are sneaking up on my life. I ask You to defend me and guard my heart against the sneaky and the not-so-sneaky attacks of the enemy. Help me to follow You no matter what. I love You. Amen.

work the Word—

Open your Bible and turn to Ephesians 6:10-20, NKJV, and learn all about clothing yourself in the whole armor of God. Verse 12 tells us, "For we do not wrestle against flesh and blood, but against principalities, against powers, against the rulers of darkness of this age, against spiritual hosts of wickedness in the heavenly places." That's why we need to put on the full armor of God. Make it a part of your daily routine. Maybe as you get ready to leave the house each morning, you mentally put on the full armor of God.

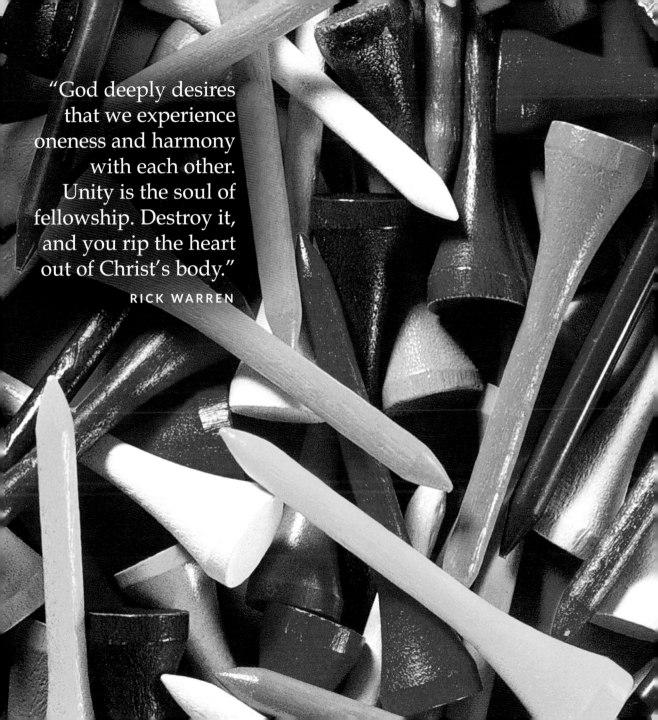

"God deeply desires that we experience oneness and harmony with each other. Unity is the soul of fellowship. Destroy it, and you rip the heart out of Christ's body."

RICK WARREN

ANDY

drawn for
DIFFERENT REASONS

THE WEEKEND AFTER EASTER, MANY EYES TURN TO A CITY IN GEORGIA. THE GREATEST GOLFERS IN THE WORLD APPROACH AUGUSTA NATIONAL TO COMPETE IN THE MASTER'S.

The gallery features people from all walks of life. Weekend golfers stroll the grounds, daydreaming about playing in the major that occurs just after Easter. Some who roam the grounds are just emphatic golf fans, there to watch their favorite player make a run for the green jacket. Golf course owners and groundskeepers attend to watch the play but also to absorb the beauty of the course.

Some attend for reasons completely unrelated to golf. To some, it is status to be at The Master's. Others come not to see famous golfers but to get close to the celebrities in attendance at the tournament.

For a week in April, Augusta captures the golf world and draws in those who will never swing a club in their life. A golf course becomes the convergence point for the rich, the common, the athletic and the unathletic, the greatest golfers in the world, celebrities, and fans of golf as well as fans of celebs.

Some follow a particular player while others remain stationary at a particular hole.

A memorable week unfolds as so many people come from a variety of places, each for a different reason. Yet it is the golf that draws them to that place. Without the golf tournament, there's no reason to travel to Augusta.

We come from different places. Our backgrounds vary and what initially drew us to Christ may even differ. Parents raised children in church and as those children grew up, they remained in the church. Others had a friend who invited them later in life and from there, they stuck in and grew to be part of the family. Some run to the church fleeing from the hopelessness of the world, discovering the hope that is Jesus Christ.

As the day of Pentecost came, the disciples gathered together. The Holy Spirit, as promised by Jesus, fell on the dedicated followers of Jesus, leading them out to proclaim the news of Jesus. People from all walks of life and from various backgrounds drew near to hear the words spoken.

The message spoke of the Lord, identifying Jesus as the hope the crowd desperately needed. The obstacle of varying languages posed no threat as God overcame the barriers so all could hear. And the Holy Spirit moved. Drawn in from different places, Jesus unified all those who heard and received Jesus as Lord.

We, too, come from different backgrounds. We come to this place and to this season in life as we are given life by the Lord. He draws us into His presence and provides us with what unifies us—Jesus Christ. The result is a collection of memorable weeks, unforgettable years, and an unimaginable eternity!

plant the Word—

"'We hear them speaking the magnificent acts of God in our own languages.' They were all astounded and perplexed saying to one another, 'What could this be?'" (Acts 2:11-12, CSB)

pray the Word—

Dear Lord, may we all be drawn together by Jesus to be in Your presence. Let us focus not on where we come from or the differences we have but let us see that it is Jesus who unites us. Bring us closer together. Call people from all walks of life to come and be a part of the body of Christ.

work the Word—

Focus on that which unifies us. So often, we think about what separates or divides us. Our focus should be Jesus. When Satan promotes what separates us, let's turn to Jesus and how only He can unite us. Remember that the cross of Jesus is big enough to cover any divide.

DID YOU KNOW?
The Waste Management Phoenix Open is the largest attended golf tournament in the world. In 2018, the tournament drew a crowd of more than seven hundred thousand during the week.

"The more you go with the flow of life and surrender the outcome to God, and the less you seek constant clarity, the more you will find that fabulous things start to show up in your life."

MANDY HALE

feed
THE BIRDS

I LOVE TO FEED THE BIRDS. OF COURSE, I FEED THE ONES THAT STICK AROUND ALL WINTER LONG, BUT WHEN SPRING ROLLS AROUND, AND ALL OF MY FAIR-WEATHERED FEATHERED FRIENDS RETURN, I REALLY KICK UP MY FEEDING GAME.

I counted just the other day—I'm up to twelve bird-feeders at our house! (Yes, I'm that crazy bird lady . . .)

Because I work from home, I am usually able to clean and refill the feeders on a regular basis, but recently, I had to be out of town because I was teaching at back-to-back writers' conferences.

Knowing the feeders would run out before I got back, I asked my husband to keep them filled while I was gone. Unfortunately, my conferences fell during tax season, and that's his busiest work season, so he completely forgot to watch over the feeders.

When I returned home, there wasn't a single seed left in any of the feeders. I felt so bad for the neglected birds, that I rushed right outside and filled every single feeder. I hoped the birds had found other feeders for feasting in my absence, and I hoped they would return even though we hadn't taken very good care of them.

Thankfully, God does a much better job taking care of us. He never forgets about us or neglects us. He never gets too busy for us. I mean, just look at the birds that live in the wild. They don't stress out about the future or store up food "just in case". God always provides. (Turns out, He doesn't really need my help feeding the birds, but I like to do my part anyway.)

Just think—if God does that for the birds, how much more will He do for His children that He created in His own image?

So, if you're worrying today, look out your window or take a walk outside and look at the birds. Take heart, knowing that God will take care of you even better than He takes care of them!

DID YOU KNOW?

Many birds eat twice their body weight in food every day. Maybe the phrase "eat like a bird" doesn't mean what it sounds like it means.

plant the Word—

"Are not two sparrows sold for a penny? Yet not one of them will fall to the ground outside your Father's care. And even the very hairs of your head are all numbered. So don't be afraid; you are worth more than many sparrows." (Matthew 10:29-31, NIV)

pray the Word—

Lord, thank You for taking care of me so well. Even though I worry sometimes, I trust You to take care of me. Thanks for loving me like You do. Amen.

work the Word—

Buy or make a birdfeeder to hang outside your window. (You can find really easy DIY birdfeeders online! One of my favorites is coating a pinecone in peanut butter and rolling it in birdseed, then hanging it on some string.) Whenever birds come by to visit, let them be a reminder of God's provision.

ANDY

the earth
WAS SHAKING

AS SUNDAY MORNING DAWNED, I HIT THE SNOOZE BUTTON TO GET AN EXTRA FEW MINUTES OF REST BEFORE LEAVING THE HOUSE TO GO TO CHURCH.

"What in the world was that?" I asked out loud, though no one else heard me.

The bed shook and windows rattled as an earthquake struck. The epicenter was about two hours from our house, but that morning will always be a day I remember because I was awakened by the earth shaking.

In the Spring of 2021, the first day of a new season, Japan shook as it was rocked by an earthquake. Most had to know it was a quake as it shook houses and businesses for hundreds of miles. The earthquake measured 7.0 and triggered tsunami warnings for the area.

Everyone notices the rumblings of the ground. With the swaying and the shaking, one's awareness rises. Something big is unfolding. Something major, a world-altering event is in the process and the effects are being felt throughout the region. The day is

anything but a normal day and that very day will be highlighted, remembered in the records because of the seismic activity.

A seismic activity broke out in Jerusalem. The day marks a celebration every year during the Spring. The event was Palm Sunday. The King of kings rode into town, presented as the Messiah, and all the city took note.

Shouts filled the air as they celebrated the One riding in on a donkey. Joy took to the streets as they believed that Jesus would deliver them from the Romans.

Palm branches waved in the air, their symbolism anything but an accident. The branches signified independence. Jerusalem shook as the Messiah entered the city. Onlookers covered the ground with their coats. Children cried out that the Son of David came. "Hosanna! Hosanna!" filled the air as a long-awaited moment finally arrived. So epic was the moment, everyone took note.

The initial shaking was followed by huge aftershocks. Palm Sunday was only the beginning of a week unlike anything the world ever experienced. He came to deliver but the deliverance was on a much deeper and eternal level than anyone imagined. And the day marks calendars nearly two thousand years later.

To celebrate Palm Sunday, we shout in adoration that the King of kings made His way to Jerusalem. We rejoice because He came to save, to deliver each of us on that day. We remember that Hope rode into town and we worship Him with thunderous joy because of that day. He journeyed closer to the cross for us.

"Doth not all nature around me praise God? I were silent, I should be an exception to the universe."

CHARLES SPURGEON

TSUNAMI HAZARD Z[O]

IN CASE OF EARTHQUAK[E]
TO HIGH GROUND OR IN

plant the Word—

"Then the crowds who went ahead of Him and those who followed kept shouting, 'Hosanna to the Son of David! He who comes in the name of the Lord is the blessed One! Hosanna in the highest heaven!' When He entered Jerusalem, the whole city was shaken, saying, 'Who is this?'" (Matthew 21:9-10, CSB)

pray the Word—

Dear Lord, let us be shaken inside from what took place on Palm Sunday. Let us shout with the fullness of our heart as we praise Jesus on this day. Make our attitude one of praise in all seasons of life as we reflect on the day that Hope entered Jerusalem and the whole city was shaken.

work the Word—

Let your voice raise high to Heaven today. There is a reason to celebrate every day, especially when we celebrate Palm Sunday. Remember the imagery of the palm branches, that they signified independence. Recognize our independence in Christ and proclaim that freedom to all who will listen.

DID YOU KNOW?
The Valdivia Earthquake in 1960 is the strongest recorded earthquake in history. It registered at 9.5.

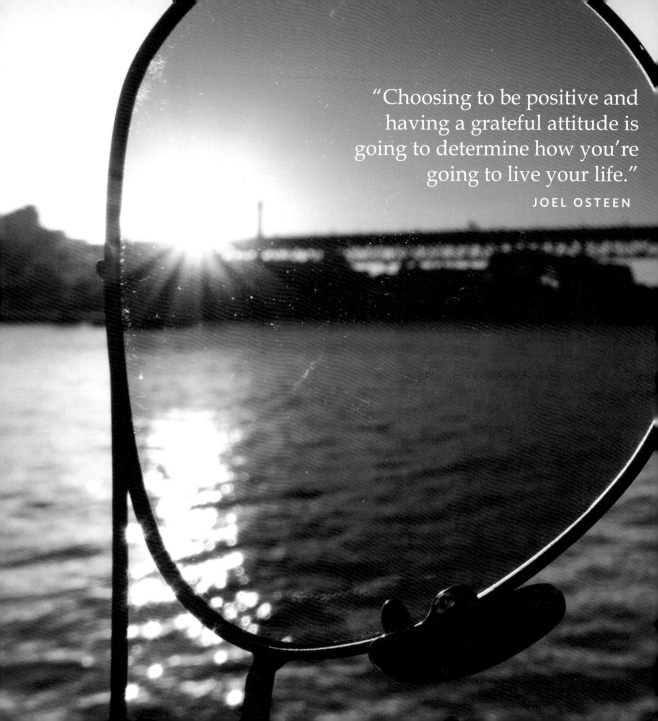

"Choosing to be positive and having a grateful attitude is going to determine how you're going to live your life."

JOEL OSTEEN

it's all about
PERSPECTIVE

SPRINGTIME IN INDIANA IS A RELATIVE TERM. OFTEN, OUR WINTERS ARE SO COLD AND SO LONG THAT PEOPLE TEND TO JUMP ON THE "SPRING HAS SPRUNG" BANDWAGON EVEN THOUGH IT REALLY HASN'T.

Seriously, if the temperature inches above 40 degrees, you'll see people walking around town in shorts, flipflops, and a sweatshirt.

Sure, their legs might be covered in goosebumps the size of Chicago, but they will shiver their way through "Spring" until it's really, officially, sprung. Not so in Florida, I discovered, when I took my oldest daughter for a campus visit to Palm Beach Atlantic University.

We ventured down to Palm Beach in early March, and just as we arrived, a cold front settled over the area. The morning of our campus tour, it was 59 degrees. It felt warm to us, since we had left snow and ice in Indiana, but the local Floridians were bundled up in layer after layer. We even saw one girl walking across campus wearing furry Uggs, a furry hat to match, gloves, and a scarf. Abby and I just looked at one another in disbelief and smiled.

I'm pretty sure that bundled-up girl believed winter had returned. Abby and I chose to believe Spring had sprung.

But seriously, it's all about perspective, isn't it?

Perspective is how we view life—day in and day out. It's easy to take the "glass half empty" mentality, but life is so much sweeter if we choose to take the "glass half full" approach. You see, when you choose to have a positive perspective, you set your life on the right path.

Of course, that's easy to say but not so easy to do, especially if you're in the habit of focusing on what's wrong in your life, instead of appreciating all that is good.

That's not to say we won't have days when we get down, but on those days, if we will meditate on our blessings and God's promises, we won't stay down for long.

It's truly a change of mindset, and it will take some practice. Just recently, I had the opportunity to practice this very thing. I was driving home from a women's retreat, and it was raining so hard that I could barely see the road. I really hate to drive in the rain. To be honest, it scares me a little, and I could have easily gone down the road of: "It's going to rain my entire drive home. The roads will probably be flooded before long. I'll never make it home before dark."

Instead, I began singing praise and worship songs. As I filled my SUV with praise, my mood began to lift, and so did the rain! It was amazing! And, to make the day even more special, God caused a double rainbow to form across the highway. It was such a gift!

Now when I have a "rainy day," I am reminded of that drive home and the rainbow that followed. Let me ask you, how's your perspective today? Is your glass half empty or half full? Are you complaining about the rain, or are you looking for the rainbow? No matter your circumstances today, keep that attitude of faith and expect good things. When you do, you'll open the door for even more blessings in your life.

plant the Word—

"So if you're serious about living this new resurrection life with Christ, act like it. Pursue the things over which Christ presides. Don't shuffle along, eyes to the ground, absorbed with the things right in front of you. Look up, and be alert to what is going on around Christ—that's where the action is. See things from his perspective." (Colossians 3:1-2, MSG)

pray the Word—

Father, help me to focus on You and Your promises when my circumstances aren't ideal. And help me to keep praising You, keeping the right perspective, and living every day as the gift it is. I love You, Lord. Amen.

work the Word—

You don't have to be a great singer to sing praises to God. Even if your songs of praise sound more like screeching cats, your melodies still please God. True worship has more to do with the condition of your heart than the quality of your voice. Why not sing a praise chorus or two today?

DID YOU KNOW?

The Bible has a lot to say about singing to the Lord. We are commanded to sing. Over and over, the scriptures say, "sing to the Lord," "sing joyfully," "sing a new song" and "come into God's presence with singing." In fact, Colossians 3:16, ESV, says, "Let the word of Christ dwell in you richly, teaching and admonishing one another in all wisdom, singing psalms and hymns and spiritual songs, with thankfulness in your hearts to God."

i've got to DO WHAT?

AT MY FIRST CHURCH, THE PREACHER'S DAUGHTER, A GIFTED YOUNG LADY, DECIDED TO DIRECT A PLAY. AS THE YOUTH PASTOR, I AUTOMATICALLY DREW A PART IN THE PRODUCTION.

My acting skills are limited. I assumed I'd be Bartholomew or maybe Nathaniel, someone who had to do very little and say even less. I learned that making such assumptions can be a bad thing.

"I want you to play the part of Jesus," she explained, a smile on her face, possibly in reaction to the immediate contortion of my face at that moment.

"You've got to be kidding me," began my response. "Have you noticed that I'm not too good at all of this?"

"You'll do fine," she said as she patted my arm.

I had no wiggle room. My boss's daughter asked me to do something. There was little option but to do it.

"One little thing," she explained further, "I want it to be as close as possible to the real Upper Room."

"OK . . ."

"I need you to wash the feet of the disciples in the play."

With that she turned away as her name was called. Immediately, those playing the disciples made jokes. They threatened to not wash their feet for a week ahead of the play, assuring the foot odor would make me gag. For weeks, they joked about it.

When the moment came in the play, it was nearly surreal to all of us. One by one they came. No one cracked a smile. The words of John 13 hit like never before in that moment.

In the Upper Room, Jesus rose from the table and took a towel. He called them to come as He took a towel and a water basin, and prepared to serve them. Matthew, Peter, Nathaniel, John, and James each came through that line and had their feet washed. In the succession, up stepped Judas. Judas Iscariot stood before the King of kings and the Lord of lords in the Upper Room and Jesus cleaned his feet.

Later that night, Jesus taught the disciples that He washed their feet as an example of what they were to do. He called them to be servants. Those leaders He called were to take the lowest position. And there stood Judas. A betrayer who once was a follower. Jesus served a meal and washed the feet of the one who would stab Him in the back. Then Jesus said, you should do the same.

The service of Jesus in the Upper Room challenges us. While we find relative ease in serving our friends and those who are nice to us, how hard is it to help those who stand as opponents?

Can we serve those who have hurt us or those who intentionally make our lives difficult?

As Easter approaches, we set out to follow Jesus's example, and He washed the feet of a traitor, a betrayer, a friend turned enemy.

In a calculated world, serve freely and serve all. The scene in the Upper Room set the stage for a life of service the world has only witnessed rarely, the first-time being Jesus. He said early in His ministry to love your enemies. Just before the cross, He set the example of serving those who mistreat you. He practiced what He preached. Do we?

DID YOU KNOW?

According to AmeriCorps, in 2018, just over seventy-seven million people volunteered their time to help organizations in America, accumulating roughly 6.9 billion hours of labor through volunteering.

plant the Word—

"So if I, your Lord and Teacher, have washed your feet, you also ought to wash one another's feet. For I have given you an example that you also should do just as I have done for you." (John 13:14-15, CSB)

pray the Word—

Heavenly Father, give us a heart like what we see in Jesus. Help us to serve all those around us just as Jesus washed the feet of His friends, as well as His betrayer. Let our service flow from a heart of forgiveness. Give us the humility to stoop down to the lowest level in order to follow Jesus in every way. Amen.

work the Word—

Being a servant is not an option for the disciple of Christ. We must serve. We long to be like Christ. Sometimes, it means we must help those who stand as enemies, those who create stress in our lives. Are we willing to do that? Will we follow Jesus to that degree?

Set aside what others have done to you. What builds your character and tells your true testimony is not the actions of others but is based on what you do. When someone hurts you, serve them. When given a chance to retaliate, stoop down and wash their feet. Jesus gave us the example, but it is our choice as to whether we listen and follow.

"There is but one just use of power,
and it is to serve people."

PRESIDENT GEORGE H. W. BUSH

"Sometimes in the winds of change we find our true direction."

UNKNOWN

MICHELLE

the wind is
ALWAYS WORKING

LAST NIGHT WE HAD A DOOZIE OF A SPRING STORM—HEAVY RAIN, HAIL, AND HIGH WINDS. THE PILLOWS ON MY FRONT PORCH BENCHES ENDED UP HALFWAY DOWN OUR STREET. AND THE SAND IN OUR FRONT YARD, WHERE THE SIDEWALK WILL SOME-DAY BE POURED (WEATHER PERMITTING), BLEW DOWN THE HILL AND INTO THE ROAD.

The wind always changes the topography of the land—sometimes subtly and sometimes quite dramatically—but it always brings change.

It certainly changed things for Noah and his family. You probably already know the story of Noah and the Ark, but just in case you're a little fuzzy on the details, here's the short version. Noah was a righteous man at a time when the world was filled with great evil. God told Noah to build an ark and gather up his family, and a male and female of all living animals, so they would be saved from the flood waters.

You see, the Lord was about to send down torrential rain to purge evil from the earth, wipe the slate clean, and start again. (You can read the full story in Genesis 5:32 to 10:1.)

While researching the story of Noah for a children's book I was writing at the time called, *Conversations on the Ark*, one verse (Genesis 8:1, NIV) stood out to me: "But God remembered Noah and all the wild animals and the livestock that were with him in the ark, and he sent a wind over the earth, and the waters receded."

Over 100 days and thirteen verses later, the earth was completely dry. The wind had obviously been at work, causing the water to recede farther every single day after God had stopped the rain, even though Noah and his family couldn't see it working.

God was in the wind, accomplishing His plan, and He still is. And when the wind blows, it changes things. It always has an effect. It always produces results. That's why I wasn't surprised when I learned the Hebrew word for wind, *ruach*, and the Greek word for wind, *pneuma*, is the same word used for "spirit." Just like the natural wind changes everything it touches, so does the Holy Spirit.

You may not always be able to see God working in your life, but He is! Remember, Noah looked out his window and saw water in all directions, but all the time, the wind was working behind the scenes to recede that water.

Over time, in God's perfect timing, that ark hit land, and Noah and his family and all of the animals exited the ark and ended the longest boat ride ever.

If you're like Noah today, and you're looking out your window and seeing water on all sides, just know that God hasn't forgotten you, and He hasn't forsaken you. Even if you can't feel Him. Even if you can't see Him. He's right there, working on your behalf, to change the topography of your life for the better. He has a good plan for you, and even if you haven't hit land yet, trust me, land is in sight! Just remember—the wind is always at work.

When it seems like nothing is happening, it can be very frustrating. It's hard to stay in faith when it appears that God isn't working, or when He isn't working fast enough for your timetable. That's why it's important to know and declare that we aren't moved by our feelings; we are only moved by our faith. Hebrews 11:1, NIV, says, "Now faith is confidence in what we hope for and assurance about what we do not see." In other words, we believe it before we see it, and we praise Him for those unseen results.

DID YOU KNOW?

The Bible mentions "the wind" in 113 verses from twenty-eight books.

plant the Word—

"'For I know the plans I have for you,' declares the Lord, 'plans to prosper you and not to harm you, plans to give you hope and a future.'" (Jeremiah 29:11, NIV)

pray the Word—

Father, I know You are always with me because Your Word promises You won't ever leave me. Help me to trust You more, even when I can't feel You; and even when I can't see You. I am excited about the plan You have for my life. Thank You for loving me through it all and working to change things for the better in my life. I love You. Amen.

work the Word—

Keep praising God for the plan He has for your life. Praise Him for the breakthrough before you see it. And keep a prayer/praise journal so you can keep track of how and when God answers your prayers. Reading back over your answered prayers will encourage you during those "long boat ride" seasons.

ANDY

a tree
WITH A STORY

FOR THOSE WHO HAVE WALKED IN FAITH FOR SOME TIME, WE HAVE AN IMAGE THAT COMES TO MIND WHEN SOMEONE MENTIONS BETRAYAL. THE NAME JUDAS ELICITS AN INSTANTANEOUS RESPONSE.

In many places, there are trees known as "The Judas Tree." Though they are generally known as redbud trees, they are given the name of Judas due to a tradition.

According to the legend, Judas Iscariot hung himself from this type of tree. After betraying Jesus and receiving the payment for his act, Judas tried to return the money, then took his own life by hanging himself. The gravity of what he did pushed him to the place where he could no longer live with himself.

The tradition of the redbud tree being called the "Judas Tree" comes from the transformation that happened after the betrayer's death. Legend holds that the blooms of the tree changed color. No longer did they bloom a brilliant, white flower but changed to color pink from that day forward.

If you're new to this legend, you are not alone. I'd never heard the legend until a friend of mine shared it with me. A few days later, an article about the trees appeared in a state magazine that further told the story. Intrigued, I learned all that I could.

Much to my surprise, the trees grew in abundance in our area. I passed them daily, yet never knew the story. They were just another bloom, just another tree adding to the festiveness of the season. The trees and their blooms captivate us, but they cause us to pause for another reason.

Judas sold out the One who he witnessed do so much. Judas was there when Jesus fed the multitude with a few loaves of bread and a few fish. With his own eyes, he saw the lame walk, the deaf begin to hear, and those with leprosy healed. He was there when Jesus opened the eyes of the blind. Judas sat in the boat as Jesus approached walking on the surface of the water.

But a moment came and the disciple turned into a betrayer. Jesus didn't set up a kingdom on earth as Judas believed He should, so Judas turned. He sold out Christ but when he realized what he did, he tried to undo his act of betrayal. He gave the money back to the ones who wanted Jesus silenced. His remorse led to his death and a tragic story that echoes today.

As we pass those trees during spring, they not only catch our eyes but give pause to our day. How are we treating our Lord and Savior today? Are we sold out to Him or are we selling Him out with how we live our lives? The blooms on the trees, according to the legend, transformed after that day, a reminder of what took place on that tree. Today, we look at that tree and are struck with this truth—live a life we do not regret.

"I have never known
a man who received
Christ and regretted it."

BILLY GRAHAM

plant the Word—

"Then Judas, His betrayer, seeing that He had been condemned, was full of remorse and returned the thirty pieces of silver to the chief priests and elders. 'I have sinned by betraying innocent blood,' he said." (Matthew 27:3-4, CSB)

pray the Word—

Heavenly Father, thank You for loving us though we often fall short. Give pause to us in this world of hustle and bustle, that we think about how we are living, what we are living for, and where we might be selling You out. Help us live a life we will not regret later.

work the Word—

Take stock of life each day. Too often, we get caught up in the running of this life so we neglect to see if we are truly running in the right direction. Stop for a few moments every day. Assess if you are serving Jesus or living for your will and expecting Jesus to bless it.

DID YOU KNOW?

The Judas Tree is native to the Mediterranean region and grows to a height of forty feet. This is the tree that many believe to be the species of tree from which Judas took his life.

"Worry does not
empty tomorrow of
its sorrows; it empties
today of its strength."

CORRIE TEN BOOM

MICHELLE

no more DREADING

FOR MANY PEOPLE, SPRING IS THEIR FAVORITE SEASON. BUT AS FOR ME? I PREFER FALL. THAT MIGHT SEEM LIKE A STRANGE STATEMENT COMING FROM SOMEONE WHO IS WRITING A DEVOTIONAL ABOUT SPRING, BUT HERE'S WHY: I AM MARRIED TO A CPA, AND SPRING EQUALS TAX SEASON FOR OUR FAMILY. IT MEANS LONG HOURS AT THE OFFICE AND STRESSFUL DAYS FOR MY HUSBAND.

Let me tell you—we have always lived for April 15th around our house! It's just part of it, and we have learned not to plan any family events in the springtime, or at least until after tax season is over. That's why every New Year's Day while the rest of the world is celebrating the beginning of a new year, I'm dreading the beginning of tax season.

But one day, when my girls were in high school, and springtime stress was ramping up, God spoke to me about this. He impressed upon my heart to stop dreading because dread is a form of fear. Maybe you're as surprised as I was to learn that dread is a form of fear, but according to Dictonary.com, dread means to fear greatly or be in extreme apprehension

of. And here's what else—it's not of God. Second Timothy 1:7 tells us that God didn't give us a spirit of fear, so if God didn't give us fear, who do you think did?

That would be the enemy.

Once I realized I was allowing the devil to rob me of my joy and replace it with dread every single Spring, I said, "Enough!" I asked God to change my perspective and replace my dread with His peace and joy. Now, I'm not saying my heart changed overnight, but it did change.

I still love Fall a bit more than Spring, but I don't dread tax season anymore. Instead, I find ways to be a blessing to my husband during his most stressful time of year, and I focus on the beauty of the season.

Maybe you have something you're dreading at this point in your life. Let me encourage you to say, "Enough!" and ask God to change your perspective so you can see things through lenses of hope, gratitude, and joy. Remember that God didn't give you a spirit of fear; He gave you the Holy Spirit to empower you and help you stand strong in every situation.

You will make it through this season and come out victorious, and God will be with you every step of the way.

Worry and dread won't change the outcome of your situation, but prayer will. So pray continually and pray effectively by praying the Word of God over whatever you're facing today. God has solutions to problems you haven't yet encountered, so stop dreading the future and enjoy whatever season you're in right now.

plant the Word—

"For the Spirit God gave us does not make us timid, but gives us power, love and self-discipline." (2 Timothy 1:7, NIV)

pray the Word—

Lord, thank You for giving me the Holy Spirit and not a spirit of fear. I trust You with what's to come, no matter what happens. I hand my dread over to You. Please replace it with Your peace and joy. I love You, amen.

work the Word—

In your journal, write some of the things you are dreading. Next, write the following scriptures underneath your worries. Begin to pray these scriptures over the situations that are causing you to worry and dread.

Psalms 55:22, CEV: "Our LORD, we belong to you. We tell you what worries us, and you won't let us fall."

1 Peter 5:7, NASB: " . . . cast all your anxiety on Him, because He cares for you."

Jeremiah 32:27, NIV: "I am the Lord, the God of all mankind. Is anything too hard for me?"

DID YOU KNOW?

Even Albert Einstein got confused and stressed out by taxes. He is quoted saying, "The hardest thing in the world to understand is the income tax," — and that's from an expert in theoretical physics!

ANDY

can they COME OUT AND PLAY?

WARMER TEMPERATURES PRODUCE A SE-RIES OF QUESTIONS, A SET THAT ECHOES THROUGHOUT THE SEASON. WINTER SHUT-TERED MOST OF THE OUTDOOR ACTIVITIES, BUT SPRING CREATES EXCITEMENT.

"Can the cousins come over and play soccer?" is the question we hear many mornings. "Can Bethany and Sammie come over?" is a request that comes each time we see their friends. "Can Grammy come over and play outside with us?" is asked every Sunday of the season.

Though there are days when we say yes, there are some days where we have to say no. Our schedules are too packed or the others are in school or Grammy is just too tired. When they run through their friends, they finally turn to us. "Can one of you go outside and play with us?"

They run around, playing with bubbles, amazed at the sizes and excited to pop them. A soccer ball emerges and they kick the ball until we can't run anymore. The slide feels the effects of a hundred trips from top to bottom and the swings enjoy their purpose for an hour.

Children love the outdoors. The feel of a Spring breeze keeps them running longer as it is more enjoyable than the oppressive summer heat. As they enjoy the outside, they want to do so with others. "The more the merrier" proves true as the group plays together on a Spring afternoon.

Many parks play host to scores of children who visit to enjoy all the park has to offer. Front yards and backyards become makeshift athletic fields and bubble lands. Laughter rises. Friendships begin and grow as the warmth of the sun intensifies the warmth of the relationships.

The worst part is when they are told they have to come in for the night.

They cannot wait to get together outside again.

Spring brings us together. The solitude of winter gives way to group activities; isolation and inactivity springs us to more involvement as opportunities expand.

"Can they come out and play?" The question is a longing of little hearts to engage with others and share in the joy life can bring.

The writer of Hebrews understood the need for community. As Christians, we need a community of believers as we walk this road of faith each day. We need them to be there during the trials of life and we get a chance to serve them by being there during their trials. One of the overlooked aspects of being a part of the church is that we get to share our joys

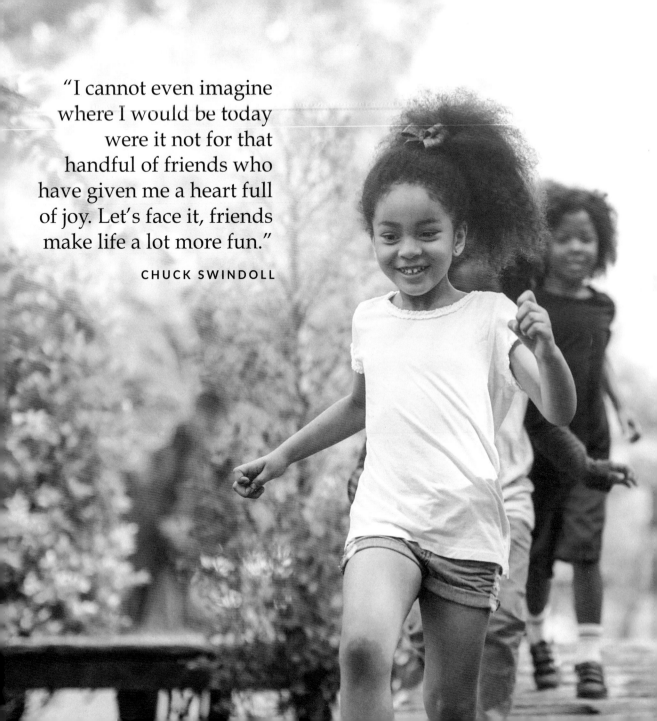

"I cannot even imagine where I would be today were it not for that handful of friends who have given me a heart full of joy. Let's face it, friends make life a lot more fun."

CHUCK SWINDOLL

with one another and share in their joys. We get to work together, serve together, pray together, and praise together.

The church gives us a chance to shake off the isolation of life and come together, share the joy of Jesus, and praise the Lord. As we pursue a higher calling in life, we rejoice in the purpose of living.

Before long, we grow so close to our faith family that we long for the next time we will be together. We choose to attend church because when we miss church, we miss being with the church. "Can they come out and play?" becomes "Can we come together and serve, pray, worship, and praise?"

DID YOU KNOW?

According to Barna research, a decline has happened in church attendance. Since 2012, the numbers have plummeted to where only three out of ten adults attend church weekly.

plant the Word–

"I rejoiced with those who said to me, 'Let us go to the house of the Lord.'" (Psalm 122:1, CSB)

pray the Word–

Heavenly Father, give us a desire to be part of the community of faith. Help us find joy in the gathering together and share in the joy of the moments of life.

work the Word–

Get plugged in to a local church. Enjoy the fellowship with others who are like-minded. Serve with others and serve the Lord with all your heart. Pray with others. Do life in community rather than isolation. Adopt the mindset that time with others of the faith is time well-spent.

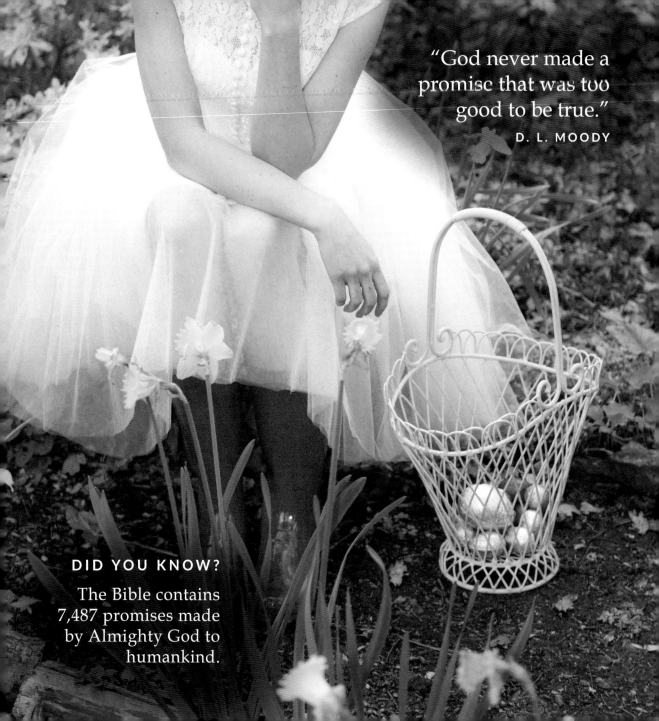

"God never made a
promise that was too
good to be true."

D. L. MOODY

DID YOU KNOW?

The Bible contains
7,487 promises made
by Almighty God to
humankind.

MICHELLE

the best easter egg
HUNTS ARE FIXED

AHHH . . . THE ANNUAL "MEDLOCK EASTER EGGSTRAVAGANZA." IT WAS TRULY A THING OF WONDER . . . ONE OF OUR FAMILY'S BEST AND MOST TREASURED TRADITIONS.

My mom, otherwise known as Mamaw, loved planning elaborate family events such as our family's Easter egg hunt. She shopped for weeks in advance, finding every grandchild's favorite candy, and several special trinkets and toys that she could stuff into each of the pastel-colored plastic eggs.

My dad, better known as Papaw, liked to get into the Easter Eggstravaganza, too, so he stuffed money into several of the plastic eggs that Mom set aside for him. In some, he put $10 bills. Others were stuffed with $5 bills. Most contained $1 bills, and a few had quarters in them.

Mamaw and Papaw not only carefully stuffed the eggs, but also, they hid them throughout their yard, under the sundeck, in flowerpots, and even in the mailbox. They knew exactly how many eggs were hidden, and they had a system in place so that every grandchild received the same amount of candy, toys, and money. They labeled each egg with a name, so if Ally found Abby's egg, she would have to put it back where she found it and go in search of her own eggs.

Of course, the grandkids were allowed to help one another find their designated eggs but they could not take each other's eggs. What a glorious plan! It made for a fun afternoon of searching, helping, finding, giggling, and celebrating.

As much as our girls loved hunting for Easter eggs in Mamaw and Papaw's yard, we figured they'd love hunting for Easter eggs at the large community event in Fort Worth, Texas, so we took them.

As Abby ran through the large field, she was outmaneuvered by faster, older children who would snatch the brightly-colored plastic eggs before Abby could grab them. This happened to Abby and Ally over and over again as they braved the bigger kids in search of their very own Easter eggs.

My husband and I were enjoying the beautiful weather, chatting with a few other parents from our neighborhood, when suddenly I heard cries of desperation from Abby, followed with gasps and sobs coming from Ally. When I found our girls, they were sitting down next to their empty Easter baskets, totally tuckered out and troubled from the unsuccessful hunt. It was at that moment it dawned on me, "They've never been to a genuine, non-fixed Easter egg hunt!"

Through tears, Abby whimpered, "The big kids took all the eggs, Mommy!"

Ally, who had found a roly poly bug to entertain her, had tear-stained cheeks and a quivering bottom lip. She was too upset to talk. As Daddy grabbed their empty baskets, I took their hands, and we all headed home. We tried to salvage the day with a quick trip to the Dollar General toy aisle and a visit to IHOP for some yummy pancakes. As I used wet wipes to remove the roly poly germs from their hands and the dirt from their little faces, I tried to explain to the girls how actual Easter egg hunts work, and how Mamaw and Papaw's Easter Eggstravaganza was "a fixed" egg hunt.

Abby looked up at me with her big green eyes and said, "Mommy, we like fixed ones best."

I'm with Abby. I like knowing when I go on an Easter egg hunt, there will be eggs awaiting me with my name on them. In fact, I like going through life like that, don't you?

That's one of the many reasons I love walking with the Lord every single day—not just on Easter—because He orchestrates my life in such a way that I feel as if I'm living out the joy, excitement, and celebration of a fixed Easter egg hunt.

When I open up God's Word and search the Scriptures, I find promises for me. And, just like the fixed Easter egg hunt, there are promises for you, too!

For example, when I read Jeremiah 29:11 that says He has a good plan for me, I can smile and say, "Yes!" and put that promise in the Easter basket otherwise known as my heart.

And so can you!

The older I get, the more I appreciate those Medlock Easter Eggstravaganzas. I look back and remember the love, enthusiasm, and care that my parents put into each Easter egg hunt, and I am assured that my Heavenly Father is even more loving, enthusiastic, and caring when it comes to His children. He has many treasures stored up for us! That's what His Word says, and I believe it, because my heart is full today.

If your Easter basket is empty this season, dive into God's Word and begin filling it with His promises especially for you.

Happy Easter, and happy hunting!

plant the Word—

"Whatever God has promised gets stamped with the Yes of Jesus. In him, this is what we preach and pray, the great Amen, God's Yes and our Yes together, gloriously evident." (2 Corinthians 1:20, MSG)

pray the Word—

Thank You, God, for loving me and blessing me. You are a good God; Your promises are true; and I am so grateful to be Your child. Amen.

work the Word—

Why not keep a personalized promise journal? Take scriptures and insert your name in them. For example, "For God has not given (insert your name) a spirit of fear and timidity, but of power, love, and self-discipline." (2 Timothy 1:7, NLT) Write those personalized promises in your journal. Memorize them. Say them over your life. And, most importantly, praise God for them!

ANDY

soil ready
FOR SEED

GROWING UP IN NORTH CAROLINA, GARDEN WORK BEGAN WHEN YOU WERE BIG ENOUGH TO PULL WEEDS.

Spring brought about the season of sowing. From corn to lima beans, potatoes to green beans, we ensured a summer and winter full of the vegetables our bodies needed so desperately.

Our family grew a garden between five families. My great grandparents, grandparents, aunts, uncles, cousins, and parents worked the land between our houses, then shared in the benefits of the labor. Four generations worked together to raise what we lived off for the summer and winter months.

My grandfather, Paw Paw Clifton, broke the ground each season. The image of him on the tractor still flashes in my mind when I pass by the place where the garden once grew. After he broke the ground, the soil sat for a few days before he came out to work it again.

The very schedule of those events was precise. He knew what he was doing. His father, my great grandfather, taught him how to work the land. My great grandfather raised a family during the Great Depression—the garden served as a lifeline.

I asked my father once, "Why does he plow it like that? Why can't we just go behind him and throw out some seed?"

"The ground has to be ready, first," my father explained. "If the ground isn't ready, the seed won't take root."

Rocks needed to be removed. The ground needed to be warm. What would result in the harvest began with the preparation of the soil before the first seed hit the dirt.

Years later, I taught on the parable of the Sower. As I read, the image of Paw Paw on his tractor rushed back.

Are our hearts the good soil? Sure, we go to church, and we read devotional books, but have we allowed God to work the soil of our soul beforehand?

In the parable of the Sower, there were four types of soil. All four soils received seed yet only one was referred to as good soil. The good soil was prepared so that it not only received the seed (the Word of God) but also produced fruit. The good soil has been cultivated by God before the first seed is thrown. These are the hearts that enter into worship, quiet time, or small groups prepared to not only hear, but to embrace the truth and to put it into action in life. These hearts allow God to tear up the surface so the Word reaches the deepest depths of this life.

Out of the four soils, only one produced something lasting. Isn't that what we want to come from our lives? When we are good soil, we receive the Word that springs up a harvest that blesses not only

"The soul can do without everything but the Word of God, without which none at all of its wants are provided for."

MARTIN LUTHER

ourselves, but also those around us, for seasons to come.

As the next Sunday rolls around, we pray for the Lord to prepare our hearts to receive His Word. We ask Him to tear up the surface of this life so that we may produce a crop that yields thirty, sixty, or even ninety-fold of what we receive from His Word.

As I think about my heart, I ask that God prepares it to be good soil. Don't we all long to see an incredible harvest come from this Sunday's worship time or from that quiet time we have today?

Remember the truth—what results in the harvest begins with how the soil is worked before the first seed hits the dirt.

plant the Word—

"But the ones sown on good ground are those who hear the word, welcome it, and produce a crop: thirty, sixty, and 100 times what was sown." (Mark 4:20, CSB)

pray the Word—

Heavenly Father, prepare my heart to receive Your Word that You might produce a crop in me that helps a world starved for hope. Amen.

work the Word—

Before a quiet time or a time of worship, take a moment to pray for a heart ready to receive the Word. Use a worship song or a time of silence to clear your mind before hearing the Word of God. Put in the work ahead of time to reap a harvest after the Word springs forth a crop.

DID YOU KNOW?
Luke features twenty-four parables of Jesus. When Jesus spoke in parables, he used topics the audience understood. He spoke of agriculture, fishing, and shepherding because those were typical careers of the common person.

"Step out today not seeking to be in the spotlight but seeking for a spot to light — be a blessing to someone."

BERNARD KELVIN CLIVE

MICHELLE

bloom in
THE SHADOWS

AS MY HUSBAND AND I WANDERED THROUGH THE LOCAL NURSERY, I CHOSE PLANTS AND FLOWERS BASED SIMPLY ON WHICH ONES I LIKED BEST, AND WHICH ONES COLOR COORDINATED BEST WITH THE EXTERIOR OF OUR HOUSE. BUT JEFF WAS QUICK TO POINT OUT OTHER CRITERIA FOR CHOOSING THE PLANTS TO SURROUND OUR NEW HOME.

It had never occurred to me that different plants require varying amounts of sunlight in order to flourish. Some require full sun, while others do better in dense shade. As we planned for our landscaping, we had to keep that information in mind and research each plant so we could place each plant in a spot where it would thrive.

You know what was interesting? Some of the most beautiful plants, such as Caladium, ferns, and Oakleaf Hydrangea do best in the shade, which is great since we have a lot of shade surrounding our house. They don't need to be in full sun all the time to bloom and flourish.

As I watch our little plants growing and thriving, I can't help but wonder where I grow best. What environment do I need to flourish? Many people believe they need to be in full sunlight—at the center of attention with all eyes on them—in order to be happy. If I'm being honest, there have been seasons in my life where I craved that sunlight and attention far too much. I needed it to feel good about myself and affirm who I was. Of course, that's not God's way. We shouldn't find our identity in the praise or attention of others; rather, we should find our identity in Christ Jesus and who He says we are.

In reality, none of us need to be in the sunlight all of the time to survive and thrive. The wisest, most content, and beautiful people I know flourish in the shadows. They are content to grow in the quiet corners, serving others unnoticed. When called upon to take centerstage and step into the spotlight, these folks rise to the occasion, but they don't need that attention to feel fulfilled.

Being the center of attention isn't a bad thing as long as we don't need it in order to be happy. We should strive to be like the shaded plants; the ferns and hydrangeas that grow beautifully in the shadows, never relying on the light. They appreciate a little light when it shines their way, but they are perfectly happy growing in a shady spot.

Think about where you're planted right now. Are you in a place where the light is always on you, or are you in a season of shadows?

For example, are you the person serving in the nursery every Sunday, or are you leading praise and worship? Are you part of a team or are you leading the team? There will be seasons of shade and seasons of full sunlight in each of our lives, but the key to thriving—and not just surviving—is to bloom wherever God has us planted at that time. Wherever you are, how could you bloom even more beautifully in the place where you're planted today?

plant the Word—

"The fear of the Lord leads to life; then one rests content, untouched by trouble." (Proverbs 19:23, NIV)

pray the Word—

Lord, please help me to be content and productive no matter where I am planted and help me to bloom no matter the season. Thank You for loving me like You do. Amen.

work the Word—

Try to perform one kind act today without posting about it on social media or telling anyone. You know, just being kind and expecting nothing in return.

DID YOU KNOW?

Begonias, common shade-growing flowers, can grow three million flowers from a single ounce of seeds. Talk about blooming wherever you're planted!

"God has a habit of using people, their gifts, and their resources to carry out His plans. In fact, we were created to be God's deputies, doing His work on earth."

DAVID JEREMIAH

ANDY

the time
IS RIGHT

BE IT FLOWERS OR VEGETABLES, SPRING BECKONS US TO PLANT. AS THE EARTH BEGINS TO SHOW SIGNS OF NEW LIFE, WE TAKE PART IN THE TRANSFORMATION.

The planting season varies, depending on where you live. Those in the deep South put seeds in the ground a month faster than those who live in the Mid-Atlantic.

Living in North Carolina, the exact date to plant is tricky. The last frost can be as early as late March or as late as mid-April.

"You can look at the Farmer's Almanac," a local farmer told me as I asked about when to put vegetable seeds in the ground.

"You use that?" I questioned, thinking he might be joking with me.

A grin shot across his face. "Yeah, I do. It's pretty accurate around here."

I decided to get a copy. I waited a few days later than the projections, afraid a frost may come as a surprise. As I studied the long-range forecast for our local weather, I knew the time had come.

"What are you doing, Daddy?" Cheyenne asked as I took seeds out to the garden.

"I'm going to plant some seeds. It's safe to plant them now," I told her as I slid out the garage door.

Little feet scampered outside behind me. She watched and thought for a minute before she asked, "Well, how do you know it's the right time?"

I explained the weather and how we could look ahead to see what the temperatures would be. I told her about the Almanac. I did my best to teach her what I learned.

"Umm . . . okay. Can I go play on the swing?"

I smiled and told her she could. I realized that I gave her an extremely long answer when really, she just wanted to go swing.

Within days, the sprouts appeared. When the ground was right and the temperatures warmed enough, a garden began growing. Spring's change opened the door for a later harvest, a blessed one that year. We just had to wait for the right time.

As we look around the world today, we see that this is the right time for Christians to sow the seeds of the gospel. Masses long for answers. Millions seek direction, guidance, and hope.

Not knowing where to find all their soul desires, they look to the world. But this is our time. Our opportunity comes as the world's promises prove untrue.

A new season arrives in our world today. Hearts stand open for good news, the good news of Jesus Christ. With every sharing of the gospel, we sow the seeds their souls are desperate to receive. The conditions have changed so drastically in our world that now is the time. Seeds of hope fall on the ears of those longing for hope. Seeds of joy fall into the hearts of those gripped by sorrow. Seeds of peace take root in souls tired of the turmoil of the times.

We have the seeds. We are the workers, the laborers for the Lord. Now is the time to plant those seeds in the lives of those around us.

plant the Word—

"Then He said to His disciples, 'The harvest is abundant, but the workers are few. Therefore, pray to the Lord of the harvest to send our workers into His harvest." (Matthew 9:37-38, CSB)

pray the Word—

Heavenly Father, send us out as workers in Your field today. Teach us how to sow the seeds that will lead to a great harvest. Just as Jesus had compassion on the crowd, move us by compassion to reach the world.

work the Word—

To the hopeless, sow the seeds of hope today. Share the hope that you find in Jesus Christ. To those longing for peace, introduce them to the Prince of Peace and tell them about the peace of God that covers your heart today.

DID YOU KNOW?

Of all the place in the United States, Alaska has one of the shortest growing seasons for plants and vegetables. Because of its location and distance from the equator, the time for growing is only about 105 days. However, Alaska benefits from times of twenty-four hours of sunlight during their growing season, which helps plants to grow large and produce crops.

"Judging others makes us blind, whereas love is illuminating. By judging others we blind ourselves to our own evil and to the grace which others are just as entitled to as we are."

DIETRICH BONHOEFFER

MICHELLE

" **bee** *"*

KIND

DID YOU KNOW THAT CARPENTER BEES OFTEN RETURN TO THE SAME NEST YEAR AFTER YEAR? I AM VERY AWARE OF THIS FACT BECAUSE THERE USED TO BE A CARPENTER BEE NEST ON THE SIDE OF OUR HOUSE (OR SHOULD I SAY IN OUR HOUSE), RIGHT NEXT TO THE PORCH.

Even though we got rid of our wood siding and replaced it with a vinyl variety, those pesky, persistent carpenter bees still hover around our house, trying again and again to get into the hole that is now covered up.

Carpenter bees are usually quite large, and they've been known to buzz you if you get too close. I'll admit it; they terrify me because I'm allergic to bees. Now, male carpenter bees don't sting—only the females are able, and they only do so if they're provoked.

But the problem is that carpenter bees look almost exactly like bumblebees, which do sting (over and over again)! Because of this, I freak out every time I see a carpenter bee—and we have lots flying around our house at the moment—so I'm in a constant state of panic whenever I go outside. No matter how many times my husband says, "They're just carpenter bees.

They won't hurt you," I still flail about and scream like a little girl. (Yep, it's pretty embarrassing.)

When we rely on perceiving the world with just our eyes, we don't always see things the way they are. Our eyes are limited. They can only reveal so much. This is true when it comes to little things, like bees, and things of great importance, like the people around us.

We often misjudge others based on their looks. A quick glance might make us think that a person is arrogant, mean, uneducated, ditzy, etc. Based on that assessment, we then assume we know that person's homelife, interests, beliefs, and attitude toward life. We might even judge whether or not we think someone is a true Christian based on appearance.

Those snap judgements and ill-conceived assumptions are so wrong.

You truly can't tell any of those things about a person with just your eyes. The only way to know what someone is like is to talk with that person. And you can't do that if you choose to run away from them the same way I run away from carpenter bees!

God doesn't care one bit about what a person looks like. What He looks at is a person's heart. When you put in the time and effort to see a person through God's eyes, you may discover a new friend.

plant the Word–

"But God told Samuel, 'Looks aren't everything. Don't be impressed with his looks and stature. I've already eliminated him. God judges persons differently than humans do. Men and women look at the face; God looks into the heart.'" (1 Samuel 16:7, MSG)

pray the Word–

God, open my eyes to those around me. Show me what You see when you look at them. Help me, Lord, to see others through Your eyes of love. Amen.

work the Word–

Here's your challenge today. Start a conversation with someone that you normally overlook. For example, why not chat with the cashier who waits on you today? Try to see that person through God's eyes. It can make a world of difference when we take time to notice someone and genuinely listen to that person. I want to do more of that, how about you?

DID YOU KNOW?
Carpenter bees can dig tunnels in wood up to ten feet long.

MICHELLE

every day
IS EARTH DAY

EVERY APRIL 22ND, PEOPLE OF ALL NATIONALITIES TAKE A BREAK FROM THEIR BUSY LIVES AND CELEBRATE EARTH DAY, AND THE MEDIA COVERS THOSE CELEBRATORY EVENTS HELD AROUND THE WORLD. FROM EARTH DAY PARADES TO TREE PLANTING INITIATIVES TO COMMUNITY CLEANUP DAY, PEOPLE OF ALL AGES DO SOMETHING POSITIVE TO IMPACT THEIR WORLD!

It's quite inspiring, really, to see people from every country joining together to celebrate this great planet.

Some choose to pick up litter on that day. Others pledge to recycle more and take better care of the planet that God has given us. Children promise to turn off lights when leaving a room in order to conserve energy, and people everywhere remember to turn off the running water while brushing their teeth in an effort not to waste water. Big or small, these changes make a positive impact.

Yes, Earth Day is important, but as believers, every day should be Earth Day. Caring for our planet and

God's creation should be part of our daily lives and an act of gratitude to our Heavenly Father who created this wonderful world for us to enjoy. Without God, there would be no beautiful waterfalls to enjoy on that Spring hike. There would be no rivers, ponds, lakes, or oceans for fishing. No hills to climb and no plants to provide the oxygen we need.

Without His creation, we wouldn't be here, either. So why not take a few moments today to praise God for all that He has created? I do this every morning when I watch the birds right outside my window. I don't make a big elaborate gesture. I just whisper, "Thank You, God, for creating such a beautiful world for me to enjoy."

When you have an attitude of gratitude, the birds' tweets will sound like a masterful hymn to your soul. The warmth of the sun will feel like a radiant hug given from the Father above. And a gentle breeze will caress you like a kiss from Heaven.

If it's been a while since you've taken time to bask in the beauty of the world around you, go ahead do that today. You don't need a special holiday to appreciate all that God has created.

Let's be thankful every day for the wonder of creation, and let's be mindful of how we might take better care of it.

"Whether it's a pebble in a riverbed or a soaring mountain peak, I see everything in the world as the handiwork of God."

THOMAS KINKADE

plant the Word—

"In the beginning God created the heavens and the earth." (Genesis 1:1, HCSB)

pray the Word—

Father, open our eyes to see the beauty and the wonder You have placed before us. Rather than overlooking the blessing, help us to immerse ourselves in it and give us a heart to do what we can to take care of what You have given to us. We love You and we are thankful for the breathtaking sights You provide on a daily basis. Amen.

work the Word—

List ways you can better take care of the planet. If you are not recycling now, why not start today? Your city might already participate in such a program, so check into it. Adopt a local body of water or a stretch of highway and keep the area beautiful by removing trash on a weekly or monthly basis. Take time to take care of what the Lord has given us.

DID YOU KNOW?

According to Dosomething.org, here are some facts about Earth Day:

• Twenty million people tuned in to a twelve-hour Earth Day Live event.

• Earth Day originated in the United States in 1970.

• In 2009, the UN designated April 22nd as Earth Day.

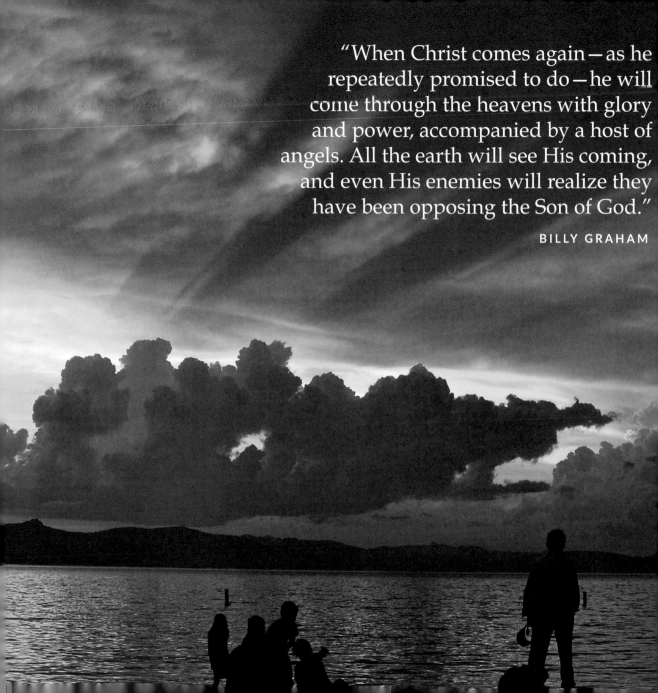

"When Christ comes again—as he repeatedly promised to do—he will come through the heavens with glory and power, accompanied by a host of angels. All the earth will see His coming, and even His enemies will realize they have been opposing the Son of God."

BILLY GRAHAM

ANDY

a streak across
THE SPRING SKY

PICTURES FLOODED THE INTERNET, ESPECIALLY ON SOCIAL MEDIA SITES, ON AN APRIL MORNING IN 2021. SOMETHING CAUGHT THE ATTENTION OF ONLOOKERS AS THEIR DAY BEGAN.

A brilliant light shot across the sky, an interruption of darkened skies yet to give way to a full morning light. The SpaceX rocket launched in Cape Canaveral, Florida, but could be seen in North Carolina. Onlookers grabbed cameras and phones to capture still shots as well as videos of the moment.

A crew left the earth that morning. It was planned. Their destination was out of this world, docking later at the International Space Station.

Amazement captivated so many as the rocket streaked across the sky. One meteorologist did a live video as the crew embarked on their journey.

The launch excited people as it was anything but ordinary. Not many days do we have a rocket ship lighting up the morning. Inevitably, some slept through it. Some never looked up to notice. But those who saw it made sure that others viewed the splendor of a moment.

The trail of exhaust divided the sky that morning. The sheer power of the rocket left its mark as it shot towards space.

The disciples were there when Jesus ascended into Heaven. They saw as He left this earth to reunite with the Father. One of those disciples, John, later received Revelation while exiled on the Isle of Patmos. What he saw then draws our eyes to the heavens each day. What is to come will be far more spectacular than a SpaceX launch.

John wrote down all he saw and heard in the Revelation. As the book tells of what is to come, how things will take place in the future, it starts with a bang. John proclaims that Jesus Himself will return and when He does, all eyes will see the moment.

The entire scene causes us to look up because at any moment, the sky could split wide, and the King of kings return.

Though some missed the space shuttle as it streaked across the sky that morning, no one will miss the day when the Lord splits the sky wide. All eyes will see Him. The return of Jesus stands as a moment we await and while we wait, we look up in anticipation. He is coming and it could happen any day.

Can you imagine that moment? The struggle of life here on Earth eases a bit with a glance towards the heavens and remembrance that Jesus isn't finished. He promised in His ministry He would come again. John saw it in the Revelation. And a day is coming when we will see it with our own eyes. One day, He will come on the clouds.

plant the Word—

"Look! He is coming with the clouds, and every eye will see Him, including those who pierced Him. And all the families of the earth will mourn over Him. This is certain. Amen." (Revelation 1:7, CSB)

pray the Word—

Dear Heavenly Father, remind us that a day is coming when we will see You. Keep our eyes trained to the sky as we endure all that the earth throws at us. When we see clouds or the exhaust of a jet, bring to our mind the reminder of Jesus' return.

work the Word—

Take a moment to look up every day. With the sight of clouds, quote Revelation 1:7. When struggles emerge, be uplifted by the promise of His coming. Use exhaust trails from jets to point others to Jesus and His return.

DID YOU KNOW?

The average speed of a space shuttle, according to space.com, is 17,500 mph.

"Where flowers bloom,
so does hope."
LADY BIRD JOHNSON

MICHELLE

april showers
BRING MAY FLOWERS

MY HOME STATE OF INDIANA IS INFAMOUS FOR CRAZY WEATHER. SOMETIMES IT SNOWS IN MAY, SOMETIMES YOU NEED SUNSCREEN IN NOVEMBER, AND SOMETIMES ALL OF THAT HAPPENS IN THE SAME DAY.

But you can always be sure that April will have many gray, rainy days. The saying, "April showers bring May flowers," is definitely true!

I'll be honest; sometimes April can be downright depressing. I always wake up hopeful that I'll see the sun, but there are many days when the sun simply can't penetrate the blanket of grayness. So, you go to bed hoping for a brighter tomorrow.

That old song, "Rainy Days and Mondays" (always get me down) by the Carpenters is spot on. Not only can rainy days keep everyone cooped up, feeling a bit trapped, but also too much rain eventually covers roads and lawns. As you can probably tell, rainy days are not my favorite.

But those rainy days seem well worth it when May comes, and the flowers begin to bloom. Sunny daffodils and vivid crocuses make you forget all about the miserable rainy days. So, even though the rain is sometimes miserable, we wouldn't have the gorgeous springtime flowers without it.

Let's face it; we all go through rainy seasons of our lives. When there are days on end that feel gloomy—and maybe even stormy—it's hard to find any joy. But we can take heart knowing that those rainy days almost always yield beautiful flowers on the other side.

Real growth takes place in the rainy seasons, and anyone who has ever had growing pains, knows that periods of growth are rarely fun but always worth it.

You know what else rainy days are great for? Reading and resting. Whether you're experiencing a literal rainy day or a spiritual one, grab your Bible and read the Psalms. Let God's Word encourage you. And don't neglect sleep. My mama used to always say, "Go to bed, honey. It'll all look better in the morning." And, you know what? She was right.

Even if my circumstances hadn't changed overnight, I always felt better in the morning. With a rested mind and body, I could see things more clearly and make better decisions. With today's technology, you can even listen to the Word of God via an app on your smartphone and fall asleep for a sweet nap.

The Bible has a lot to say about sleep, but here's a verse I really like: "My son, do not lose sight of these—keep sound wisdom and discretion, and they will be life for your soul and adornment for your neck. Then you will walk on your way securely, and your foot will not stumble. If you lie down, you will not be afraid; when you lie down, your sleep will be sweet." (Proverbs 3:21-24, ESV)

Just remember, those rainy days are making you wiser and stronger. See them as an opportunity to deepen your relationship with God. Ask Him to help you look past those dark clouds. There just might be sunny, happy, exciting opportunities in tomorrow's forecast.

plant the Word—

"Consider it pure joy, my brothers and sisters, whenever you face trials of many kinds." (James 1:2, NIV)

pray the Word—

God, I ask that You use my struggles for Your ultimate good. If it's Your will, I also ask that You reveal to me the blessings that emerge from this time of trial. I will trust You no matter what. Amen.

work the Word—

Once the rain has cleared and it's safe, go for a walk in a park or hiking trail and search for Spring flowers, remembering that they have grown because of the rain. Whenever you find flowers, think of a way that God has used your trials for good.

"They tell me revival is only temporary; so is a bath, but it does you good."

BILLY SUNDAY

a full week IN THE OLD COUNTRY CHURCH

THE LIFE OF ANY BAPTIST IN THE 1980'S IN- CLUDED CERTAIN ASSURANCES. WE CREAT- ED REASONS TO MAKE A CASSEROLE FOR A COVERED DISH LUNCH AT LEAST ONCE A MONTH. AN ANNUAL HOMECOMING SER- VICE BROUGHT PEOPLE FROM FARAWAY PLACES, AND EVERY SPRING, WE HAD A WEEKLONG REVIVAL.

My mother believed that if the doors of the church opened, we had a standing reservation to be there. When revival week came, I knew what my week entailed. School during the day. Homework as soon as I got home. Church every night. Perhaps that's why I became a pastor.

I cannot recall the names of the preachers that spoke during those revival weeks. I cannot recall the details of every message given over the course of the weeks, but one thing stood out—the presence of the Holy Spirit ran through that place.

"Hurry up and eat supper. We've got to get to church," Mom hastened as my sister and I sluggishly worked our way through the evening.

"Do I have to go?" one of us inevitably asked, thinking somehow she changed her mind from the night before.

"Yes, you do have to go . . . and I will not be late."

A groan or two filled the air until she put a stop to that by retelling how Jesus had to die for us so the least we could do was spend an hour at revival.

Once we arrived at church, we enjoyed being there. Hymns rang out from voices joyous about the time of worship. The preacher gave rousing messages and the shouts of "Amen" and "Hallelujah" reinforced to us a point that resonated in the congregation.

Fewer churches have the Spring revival anymore. Those who do feature a half-week revival now. Maybe it's because we are all too busy to give up a full week. Maybe it's that attendance dropped so drastically during the week a decision was made to shorten it. But looking back, I thank God for those weeklong revivals of my past.

The very nature of revivals whisks the modern church back to the days of the early church. After the day of Pentecost, the body of believers didn't wait a week to get together.

If you read in Acts, they gathered together every day. A longing existed within them to absorb more. They shared the stories of Jesus, they praised, they rejoiced, and they ate meals together. Could you imagine the prayer services of that day? They brought their friends with them and more people came to know Christ as a result!

What if we stopped limiting God to an hour or two each week? The early church didn't watch the time of day but stared at the movement of the Spirit. Those old revivals served a point even If I didn't understand it at that time. Those weeks were the chance to step deeper into what God was doing by opening the doors more often.

plant the Word—

"Every day they devoted themselves to meeting together in the temple complex, and broke bread from house to house. They ate their food with a joyful and humble attitude, praising God and having favor with all the people. And every day the Lord added to them those who were being saved." (Acts 2:46-47, CSB)

pray the Word—

Heavenly Father, draw us into Your house more than a time or two a week. Give us a longing to be in that place. Show us what You can do when we set aside everything else to worship You. Fill us with a desire to want more.

work the Word—

Extend the dedication of life beyond Sundays and Wednesdays. Start up a Bible study in your home, encourage new gatherings at your church. Join others for prayer and set a few extra chairs around the dinner table. Let God work beyond one hour of the week. Give Him the whole week.

DID YOU KNOW?

The Los Angeles Crusades sparked the Lord's work through Billy Graham's ministry. Originally planned for three weeks, the movement of the Holy Spirit kept them hungering for more, extending to fifty-seven days.

one wrong
STEP AND ... SPLASH!

SPRINGTIME BECKONS US TO GO OUTSIDE AND ENJOY ALL THAT NATURE HAS TO OFFER. AND, WHEN IT CALLS, MY HUSBAND AND I PUT ON OUR WALKING SHOES AND HEAD OUTSIDE. WE ABSOLUTELY LOVE TAKING WALKS AND HIKES TO GET IN OUR CARDIO BUT ALSO TO ENJOY THE BEAUTY OF SPRING.

Since moving to our newly-renovated home that backs up to the woods, we discovered we can access the Milwaukee Trail, an old railroad line turned into a beautiful fitness trail, anytime we want because it's directly behind our house. However, it's not as simple as it sounds.

Though the trail is near, to get to the trail, we have to cross a creek. The running waters are not a rushing river but enough of an obstacle that we have to plan to cross it—especially if we've had a very wet Spring.

On this particular day, my husband navigated it first, setting up rocks along the way so I could cross the cold waters without getting my feet wet. The plan seemed perfect, but one thing was not considered . . . my inability to keep my balance. A former cheerleader and gymnast, my balance helped me excel earlier in life . . . my lack of balance on that day, however, accelerated my descent into the frigid waters.

Though my hero of a husband had laid out a way for me to pass over the creek without getting wet, my clumsiness landed me smack-dab in the middle of the creek.

Jeff and I laughed about the whole ordeal as we continued our walk on the Milwaukee Trail, my soggy shoes squeaking with every step. I'm not sure how much cardio I got in that day, but my abs definitely got a workout from all of the laughter.

That day was a good reminder that life doesn't always turn out exactly as we plan. The question is: What do we do when the plans we make fail? Do we give up or do we get up?

If all we do is give up when life falls out of balance, we will never see what can come with a little persistence.

We could have mailed it in that day, but we chose to keep pressing on, enjoying the moment even if it went off-script. We had a great time just being together, even if my feet were a little squishy.

It's important to remember that our plans are just that—ours. God may have other plans. Sometimes, things go awry, but even in that, we can choose to see what God is teaching us through those mishaps and simply enjoy the journey.

The next time you fall down (whether figuratively or literally), get up, dust yourself off, and slosh forward knowing there is something beautiful to behold on the other side of the creek.

"Don't give up . . .
don't ever give up."

JIM VALVANO

plant the Word—

"Do not remember the past events, pay no attention to things of old. Look, I am about to do something new; even now it is coming. Do you not see it? Indeed, I will make a way in the wilderness, rivers in the desert." (Isaiah 43:18-19, HCSB)

pray the Word—

Heavenly Father, implant a resilient spirit within us. Just as You never gave up on us, help us not to give up when our plans don't go as we'd hoped. Teach us to laugh. Push us to press forward. Show us how to praise You when life goes well, and on the days when we slip and fall in the creek. Amen.

work the Word—

Find the ability to praise God in the mishaps. See disruptions as a chance to laugh at life, a chance to pause in the commotion, and a chance to be grateful and joyful in all things. Grab your journal and describe a time your plans went totally awry . . . what did you learn from that experience? Did you make a great memory?

DID YOU KNOW?

Thomas Edison, in inventing the light bulb, originally believed the project to be a three- to four- month process. The final count was fourteen months.

"I have one desire now —
to live a life of reckless
abandon for the Lord,
putting all my energy
and strength into it."

ELISABETH ELLIOTT

ANDY

growing CLOUDS, A RUMBLE IN THE DISTANCE

IN THE DISTANCE, THE ONCE BLUE SKIES SHOW A CHANGE IN COLOR. SOMETIMES, IT IS GRADUAL, GROWING A LITTLE DARKER OVER AN HOUR. OTHER TIMES, THE BLACK CLOUDS APPEAR TO BUILD WITHIN SECONDS.

During the spring, thunderstorms can pop up anywhere and can be intense. Tornadoes spin out of ominous clouds. Severe thunderstorms leave behind hail and wind damage, often times flooding low-lying areas with intense rainfall. One of the sounds of spring is the rumbling of thunder as hot and cold collide in the air.

In 2011, the instability led to a tornado outbreak in the Southeast. We watched in horror as coverage came from places like Tuscaloosa, Alabama, the destruction beyond imagination.

"Okay, guys, we are heading south," I told our students.

"Where? What are we going to do?" voices asked as their curiosity led to excitement and questions.

"We are going to Tuscaloosa to help clean up after the tornadoes," I told them.

Immediately, they began discussing what they thought we could do to help. We saw the pictures online and saw the images on the television. No picture or video could prepare us for what we saw there.

For a week, we worked . . . hard. That Spring turned the lives of those residents upside down but helped our world turn right side up. We listened as the Lord sent us to where the needs were. God moved us into their brokenness, helping us to understand Jesus's heart and method for ministry. A decade later, those who went on the trip still talk about the events of the week.

A man sat near a pool. He needed healing but so did the others gathered around that very pool. An angel stirred the waters and the first to enter the water received healing. The man, according to John, struggled with his illness thirty-eight years. Jesus asked the man if he wanted to be healed and when the man answered, he explained his situation.

Others reached the water before him. Some of the sick there had someone to help them into the pool. This man had no chance to reach the waters, but he was about to learn that the Living Water, the Healer, came to where he was. With one command, the lame man stood up. Jesus healed the man who once wondered if he'd ever walk again.

But let's not miss this. Jesus could've healed him from another region. But Jesus went to where the man lay. He walked among the sick and the broken. He went where He was needed the most.

This Spring, we have the chance to be like Jesus. We can go to where the hurting and the broken reside. We can be ministers on the move, addressing the needs of those in need, doing so for the glory of the Lord. Let's be there in their storm and once it passes, we can help them put everything back together.

plant the Word—

"When Jesus saw Him lying there and knew he had already been there a long time, He said to him, 'Do you want to get well.'" (John 5:6, CSB)

pray the Word—

Our Loving Father, thank You for meeting us where we are in life. When storms strike, You are there. When our lives are shattered, You are there to pick up the pieces. Take us to the places where others are in need. Teach us how to be Your hands and feet to those in need in this world.

work the Word—

Identify the needs of those in your community and beyond. Target the needs and go to meet those needs where they are. Look at areas that feature high homeless rates and take warm meals. When storms strike, go to those who are trying to rebuild. See the needs and be moved to go to those needs.

DID YOU KNOW?
The April 27, 2011, Super Outbreak of tornadoes caused an estimated $10 billion worth of damage in the south. A decade later, some places are continuing to rebuild.

springtime
SCENTS

DO YOU EVER JUST STEP OUTSIDE AND SAY, "IT SMELLS LIKE SPRING TODAY?" THE ARRIVAL OF SPRING BRINGS WITH IT SO MANY AMAZING SMELLS BECAUSE EVERYTHING IS FRESH AND NEW AND ALIVE.

There's the earthy scent of freshly-cut grass. There's the sweet fragrance of daffodils and lilac. And the aroma of cool, fresh rain.

Maybe there are some specific smells that bring back Spring memories for you. Whenever I drive by a baseball field in the Spring, I am taken right back to my high school days when I served as one of two "bat girls" for our Bedford North Lawrence Stars Varsity Baseball team. In a moment, it's 1987 and I am back in that dugout. Certain smells can evoke vivid memories, more so than any other of our five senses.

Our sense of smell is very powerful. In fact, it's actually the strongest human sense, foundational to the way we experience the world. Though we have come to rely more on our ability to see in most situations, our nose is quite remarkable. A 2014 study showed that humans can distinguish at least 1 trillion different odors! And a 2015 study showed that everyone has a scented fingerprint. In other words, we all have a distinct smell.

Well, guess what? As Christians, we also have a distinct smell. The Bible says we are the aroma of Christ. When we spend time with God and allow Him into our hearts, His presence begins to emanate off of us like a sweet aroma. We should be a breath of fresh air when we enter the room.

People should notice there's a different essence about us. They may even begin to ask what it is that makes us so different — so full of unconditional grace, love, and joy.

So go out and be so deeply invested in Christ that you can't help but carry His aroma. Be that breath of fresh air everywhere you go.

"Live simple, love
well, and take time
to smell the flowers
along the way."

MARK TWAIN

plant the Word—

"For we are to God the pleasing aroma of Christ among those who are being Saved and those who are perishing. To the one we are an aroma that brings death; to the other, an aroma that brings life. And who is equal to such a task? Unlike so many, we do not peddle the word of God for profit. On the contrary, in Christ we speak before God with sincerity, as those sent from God." (2 Corinthians 2:15–17, NIV)

pray the Word—

Lord, cover me with Your fragrance. Fill me with Your Spirit so Your presence emanates from me everywhere I go. Amen.

work the Word—

In one interaction you have today, make it your focus to intentionally radiate with God's grace and love. And while you're out, enjoy the smells of Springtime! Go ahead. Take a deep breath.

DID YOU KNOW?

Spring air has so much fragrance because the warm, humid air can hold more molecules carrying scents. In fact, flowers smell best just before or after a rain because moisture in the air helps the aroma molecules travel.

"God is unchanging. The weather changes. Fashion changes. Even change changes. God has not changed and cannot and will not ever change."

MAX LUCADO

unusual sight
IN AN UNUSUAL YEAR

FOOTBALL TYPICALLY KICKS OFF IN SEPTEMBER AND WINDS DOWN LATER IN THE FALL. BUT 2021 STARTED AS UNUSUAL AS 2020 ENDED, A CONTINUATION OF A YEAR THE WORLD SHUT DOWN.

Sure enough, in April of 2021, I sat in the stands on Homecoming night to see my high school team play football. An unusual feeling filled the stadium. For one, the game was played outside the normal season. Normally, Homecoming games take place on chilly nights in late October or early November. On this night, it was in the seventies, the sun was far from setting, and I even began sweating.

My mind recalled my years at the school, those Friday nights in the stands, under the lights. I could almost hear the voices from way back when, the cheering of the cheerleaders, the sound of the band playing the fight song or the theme from *Hawaii Five-0*.

But I couldn't shake the vibes of a night that felt out of place.

A pandemic flipped the script on life and on high school football. The world turned upside down. Head scans and masks accompanied a ticket for admission. Securing a ticket took place online, not at the ticket booth at the front gate.

Something felt off. For a moment, despair set in as the changes taking place were called by some "the new normal." The sight shook my core because of the drastic shifts we endured for more than a year. I looked around and wondered what other changes and shifts might come down the road.

The world constantly changes. If one thing is certain, it's change. We experience instability on a global scale and the pandemic brought instability to every community. Each week, there were different guidelines.

"Will anything stay the same?" a friend asked, the desperation of life's overhaul a little too much to bear anymore.

"Doesn't seem like it . . . " I responded as I focused solely on what I saw on television and what I saw around me.

Truth is, One doesn't change. His name is Jesus Christ and in our inconsistent world, He remains the same. The standards of the Lord do not change.

The presence of the Lord is unwavering to the righteous and the truth of the Lord never needs an update. The writer of Hebrews reminds the reader that in an uncertain world, Jesus is certain. Who He is never changes with the times so we stand boldly in Him. He is who He has been and who He will be.

Uncertainty leads to fear. When we lean on society, we feel the insecurity of a world constantly swaying. But Jesus is our Rock and when He is the Rock of our lives, we no longer fear. We praise the One who is, who was, and He who will be forevermore—the consistent Savior of an inconsistent world.

plant the Word—

"Jesus Christ is the same yesterday, today, and forever." (Hebrews 13:8, CSB)

pray the Word—

Dear Lord, thank You for the consistency we find in Jesus Christ. As the world shifts the standards of life by the week, we praise You that You are unchanging. Remind us of the stability that we find in You. Ease our fear by refocusing our eyes to our faith in You.

work the Word—

Go through Scripture and learn more about the nature of the Lord. Keep a visual reminder of His unchanging love, new mercies each day, and the astounding reach of His grace. When you hear others talking about the changes, point them back to Jesus and His unchanging nature.

DID YOU KNOW?
Because of the uncertainty of the pandemic, Wall Street had one of its worst days on March 16, 2020. The Dow dropped 2,997 points that day.

MICHELLE

adopted into
THE FAMILY

EVERY APRIL 30TH, THE UNITED STATES CELEBRATES ADOPT A SHELTER PET DAY, BUT WE DON'T WAIT UNTIL THAT DESIGNATED DAY AROUND OUR HOUSE TO CELEBRATE OUR BELLA MARIE. WE ADOPTED BELLA FROM THE WHITE RIVER HUMANE SOCIETY FIVE YEARS AGO.

That's the day she chose us.

I'll never forget that snowy Spring morning. I had made plans to go to the local humane society with my friend Bethany in hopes of finding her a dog. She'd been considering adopting a dog for a while, and I was sure I'd found the perfect pooch for her. You see, I'd been volunteering at the humane society on Saturdays and had fallen in love with a sweet black and white dog whose owner had surrendered her just a few days before. In fact, I secretly wanted to adopt her, but I knew my husband Jeff would be against it since we already had a long-haired dachshund and two cats.

The roads were a bit slick that morning, so I asked Jeff if he would drive us in his truck. He agreed and off we went.

"You're going to love her," I told Bethany, as we signed in at the White River Humane Society's front office. While Jeff parked the truck, I headed back to get sweet Bella.

"Hey girl," I called to Bella as I approached her cage. "You ready to meet your new owner?"

Bella ducked her head and hid behind my legs. No matter what Bethany did, Bella wouldn't come to her.

"She's new to the shelter," I explained. "She's just really scared. She'll warm up to you."

Just then, Jeff walked through the door. Bella took one look at him and leapt into his arms. My friend whispered, "I think she's your dog."

She was right. The very next day, we made it official and adopted Bella, and she has been a big part of our family ever since. Rescue dogs are precious. It's like they know they have been given a second chance at life, and they show how thankful they are every single day.

Bella and I have that in common. I am thankful every single day that Jesus rescued me and gave me a second chance.

If you're a Christian, I bet you feel the same way. When I was lost, God loved me enough to save me. He sent His only Son to die on a cross for my sins so that I could have an eternal home. And He did the same for you!

"If there are no
dogs in Heaven,
then when I die I
want to go where
they went."

WILL ROGERS

Oh, and I hope you'll consider adopting a shelter dog or cat if you're thinking of adding a new pet to your household. You just might find your Bella there.

plant the Word

"God decided in advance to adopt us into his own family by bringing us to Himself through Jesus Christ. This is what he wanted to do, and it gave him great pleasure." (Ephesians 1:5, NLT)

pray the Word

God, thank You for loving me and adopting me into Your family. I love You. Amen.

work the Word

I've never regretted investing my time in helping animals. Whether working at an animal adoption event or asking for donations for a humane society fundraiser, I've always loved helping those sweet creatures who can't help themselves. If you'd like to join me, why not reach out to your local humane society, and ask how you can get involved? Most animal shelters rely on volunteers to help with laundry, clean the cages, do the dishes, walk the dogs, and more. But, if you're taxed for time, maybe consider making a monetary donation or dropping off some dog and cat toys, kitty litter, bleach, towels, blankets, dog beds, animal crates, etc.?

DID YOU KNOW?

Approximately 6.5 million companion animals enter shelters nationwide each year. And about 3.2 million of those animals (dogs and cats) are adopted each year.

"A man may hear a thing and, as we say, it goes in one ear and out the other, and so it often does, but that which a man gets in his mouth till he tastes it, and it is sweet to his palate, well, he has truly received that."

CHARLES SPURGEON

ANDY

drop
OF GOODNESS

THE BEES OF SPRING PERFORM THEIR JOB WHICH GIVES US A MOMENT OF JOY AS CHILDREN.

Our days in May were never wasted indoors. Our parents ran us out of the house in the morning, and we never objected to their suggestions to go outside.

The hours flew by as we trekked our way through the woods, exploring all nature had to offer. One of the greatest discoveries came near the tree line by our old dirt road.

"Hey man, look over there," my cousin said as he pointed towards that tree line. "There's a bunch of honeysuckles."

I looked over but had no idea what he was talking about. "Yeah, man . . . umm, what is a honeysuckle?"

"Those white things. If you pull on the stem, a drop of honey comes out."

"Awesome," I replied, following him towards the abundance of blossoms I'd never paid attention to before.

He reached down to pull the bloom, showing me how to do it myself. Sure enough, when he pulled the stem down, there sat a single drop of honey. I stood amazed that he was actually telling the truth.

"Try it," he said as he reached for another. A hint of sweetness led to us to pulling off dozens of blooms that afternoon.

The moment stands fresh in my mind. Though three decades have passed, I can still taste the sweetness of those little drops of honey. Our family sold the house, clearing took place thereafter, and when I returned years later, the row of honeysuckles had long been cleared away. The tree line only remained in the recollections of my mind as where it once stood now pastured horses.

But I remember.

The taste and the smell, accented by the joy of discovery, chiseled the moment in my mind. Though everything about the place changed, the memory remained.

Life features so many changes, some of which can be bitter to swallow. But the Word of God remains sweet and unchanging.

The psalmist spoke of the sweetness of the Word of God. The satisfaction of the Word of God is sweeter than honey. From the Bible comes the wisdom that provides understanding, the understanding that leads to meaning, the meaning that gives us value in life. From the Word of God, light bursts forth as the darkness cannot stand and the Word gives of the flavor of true life.

The very blessing of the Word is that its flavor holds over time. A verse comes as sweet to the lips when life leaves us parched. The sweetness of the Word is never forgotten as it nourishes and excites the soul years after the Word is received.

Has life lost its flavor to you? Spring open the Word of God and feed on a Psalm or a Proverb today. What the depths of your soul desires, the Word of God provides.

plant the Word—

"How sweet Your word is to my taste—sweeter than honey in my mouth. I gain understanding from Your precepts; therefore I hate every false way." (Psalm 119:103, CSB)

pray the Word—

Heavenly Father, give us a longing for the sweetness of Your Word today and every day. Remind us that Your Word is what nourishes our souls like nothing else in this world.

work the Word—

Find time to savor the Word of God today. Too often, we rush through reading the Bible so we can get on to other aspects of life. Today, clear your mind and your schedule. Truly absorb the depth of the Bible. Let it be on your lips every day as you absorb more and more each day.

DID YOU KNOW?
In the United States, in 2017, honey-producing colonies of bees produced over 1.4 million pounds of raw honey.

MICHELLE

sunshine
AND WATER

SCROLLING THROUGH FACEBOOK ONE AFTERNOON IN EARLY MARCH LAST YEAR, I CAME ACROSS AN ADVERTISEMENT FOR THE NIFTIEST LITTLE GADGET. IT WAS A SMALL DISC THAT YOU PLACED IN YOUR BIRDBATH, AND ONCE THE DISC WAS FULLY IMMERSED, IT CREATED A BEAUTIFUL LITTLE FOUNTAIN. BEING THE BIRD LOVER THAT I AM, I JUST HAD TO HAVE IT, SO I ORDERED IT.

Several months passed before it showed up at my doorstep. In fact, it had taken so long, I'd forgotten all about it until I opened the package.

Once I realized what it was, I couldn't wait to try it out in the birdbath in our backyard. But I figured I'd better read the instructions first to make sure I put it together correctly. That's when I saw it . . . all of the directions were written in Chinese. Thankfully, there were pictures showing how to assemble it, so I was pretty sure I'd put it together correctly.

With the little disc in hand, I bolted for the backdoor and headed straight for our cute little birdbath. I immediately dropped the disc into the half-filled birdbath and waited for the little fountain to spray. I waited . . . and waited . . . and waited.

Nothing. Not even a spritz.

Figuring I must've put it together wrong, I marched back into the house and hollered for my hubby. Jeff was good at mechanical things. I was confident he could figure out what I'd done wrong. He looked at the disc and then at the pictures on the instructions.

"It looks like you did it right," he encouraged. "Let's go try it."

"I already did that, and it didn't work," I explained.

Still, he headed for the backyard with the disc in hand, and I followed.

He dropped it into the water, just as I had, and then he grabbed the hose.

"You have to immerse the disc in the water. You didn't have enough water before," he said, matter-of-factly.

I watched and waited.

Still . . . nothing.

"I think it's broken," I said.

"What'd you pay for it?" Jeff asked.

"It was $19.99, plus shipping and handling," I answered.

"Well, you get what you pay for," Jeff said, smiling.

Disappointed, I just left the disc in the birdbath, figuring I'd throw it away the following day. The next morning, I sat down to have my devotions and looked out over our backyard, just taking in the morning sun. That's when I noticed the fountain. It was working! And it was beautiful!

"Keep your face to
the sun and you
will never see the
shadows."

HELEN KELLER

I rushed outside, in my nightgown, to take a look up close. Sure enough, the little fountain sprayed just like it had in the video I'd seen on Facebook. In just a few minutes, Jeff joined me outside and we both watched the little fountain shooting water into the air.

"How'd you fix it?" he asked.

"I didn't. It just magically started working all on its own."

That's when Jeff had his "aha moment."

"It's solar powered!" he said.

He was right. When the sun poured into our backyard that morning, it activated the lovely little fountain.

As it turned out, the fountain wasn't broken. It was designed to work only when immersed in water and basking in the sun. When those two things were present, the disc made a gorgeous little fountain.

We're a lot like that little disc fountain. We only truly work when we are immersed in water, which is the Word of God, and when we're basking in the Son, Jesus Christ.

When we let God's Word wash over us, and we spend time in the presence of Jesus, we are transformed from a plain little disc to an active fountain that bubbles over with the very essence of God. When we neglect reading the Bible and spending time with Jesus, we are not effective and appear broken to a world that so desperately needs the Jesus we have living on the inside of us. So, go ahead. Get in the Word and step into the Light today. Before long, your little fountain will make a big splash for the Kingdom of God.

plant the Word—

"Whoever believes in me, as the Scripture has said, 'Out of his heart will flow rivers of living water.'" (John 7:38, ESV)

pray the Word—

Father, help me yearn for Your Word and Your presence. Please fill my heart with your love, joy, and peace so that it will bubble out of me onto all I encounter. I love You, Lord. Amen.

work the Word—

As a reminder of this fountain devotion, why not create your own DIY water feature/bird bath for your own backyard? There are many tutorials online. I found this one on YouTube: www.youtube.com/watch?v=E5p46gQ_5OY that uses clay pots. Enjoy!

DID YOU KNOW?

Early bird baths were just simple depressions in the ground or in a tree. It wasn't until the 1830s that a bird bath as we know it was invented by UK garden design company, Abrahm Pulman & Sons.

"Words which do not give the light of Christ increase the darkness."

MOTHER TERESA

green sparks
IN THE NIGHT

A FLASH OF GREEN LIGHT DRAWS OUR ATTENTION. THE FLASH PIERCES THE DARKENED NIGHT, IF ONLY FOR A BRIEF MOMENT.

Springtime promises the arrival of fireflies, or as we call them down south, lightning bugs. The critters light up a Spring night, capturing the attention of all who see the brief disruption of the increasing darkness of night.

As children, the coming of lightning bugs injected joy every Spring. We used a nail, or a knife, to pierce holes in the top of a Mason jar lid. Once the small holes were made, we ran through the yard catching the lightning bus and putting them in our jar.

Their flashing lights inside the jar made for a makeshift lantern, one we could enjoy for a little while. I normally sat mine on the patio wall and stared at it for a bit. Eventually, we unscrewed the top to allow the bugs to fly away again.

As my daughters grew up, I began to take them outside to experience the joy of catching lightning bugs.

"I got one, Daddy," Autumn called out, her smile lighting up the night much like the little bug in her hand.

"You sure did. Be careful not to smash him."

My attention turned to my oldest daughter. She carefully snuck up on her target.

"Look, Daddy. I caught one, too," she called out after making her first catch.

"Good job, honey."

For thirty minutes or more, we chased and caught them together. Every time I said it was time to go inside, they groaned and begged to catch just one more.

Just as the fireflies light up a night in the Spring, Jesus told the crowd gathered on the hillside to go out and light up the world. He told them to let their light shine so that others could see and through that, the Father received glory.

The darkness of the world remains intact today as it was that day Jesus spoke. Just as it suffocated so many when Jesus delivered the Sermon on the Mount, so it threatens even unto today. The Light of the world told us to be lights in this world.

The darkness seems vast, but each piercing of that darkness draws the attention of others. Little lights that shine offer hope that daylight will come and joy as darkness' grip is loosened. Before long, lights combine to illuminate the night even more.

Let your light shine every day for Jesus. Our world longs to see a little light in these times and the light of Christ shines in us.

By shining today, someone else may find hope and joy tonight. A lightning bug without the light is just another bug. What sets it apart is the way it glows. What sets us apart is the way we glow for the Lord every day of our lives.

plant the Word—

"No one lights a lamp and puts it under a basket but rather on a lampstand, and it gives light for all who are in the house. In the same way, let your light shine before men, so that they may see your good works and give glory to your Father in heaven." (Matthew 5:15-16)

pray the Word—

Dear Heavenly Father, help us to shine for You and bring You glory through our lives. Keep us focused on righteousness and help us to inspire others to draw closer to You. We long to pierce the darkness of these times.

work the Word—

Radiate the hope that is in you each and every day. Be the light of Christ regardless of where you are. Speak the words of truth. Use your hands to do the work of the Lord. Share what He has given you so that others see Him in your life.

DID YOU KNOW?

Fireflies' light is the most efficient light in the world. According to Firefly Conservation and Research, 100 percent of the energy is emitted as light while many other sources of light only emit about 10 percent of their energy as light.

ANDY

senior
SKIP DAY

AN ANNUAL TRADITION AT OUR HIGH SCHOOL MEANT ONE DAY A YEAR, THE SENIOR CLASS BAILED ON SCHOOL FOR A DAY, ONE CAREFULLY SELECTED EARLIER IN THE YEAR. ON "SENIOR SKIP DAY," GROUPS OF STUDENTS CUT CLASS TO GO TO THE LAKE, GO TO THE MOVIES, OR TO GATHER AT A HOUSE WITH A SWIMMING POOL. AS STUDENTS, WE LOOKED FORWARD TO THE DAY FOR THREE YEARS.

As skip day approached my senior year, we decided to keep it local. A friend had a swimming pool, so the plan was to get together, go and get breakfast, then go to his house and hang out. The day, however, did not go as planned.

Some faculty members, whether by chance or by hearing of the plan, thwarted what we scheduled. We ended up having quizzes and tests that were assigned in a few classes. We cut part of the day, playing basketball and going swimming. But as fifth period approached, dispersion from our gathering began.

"I've got to go to school," I told Michael. "I've got a Physics quiz and I can't afford to fail anything."

"I've got a Calculus exam," another one of our friends commented, making his way to his car.

I had no desire to go back on campus that day. In fact, no one did. However, what it would cost us in the long run wouldn't be worth the short-term pleasure. Most of us would not have been able to dig out of the hole a zero would have dug for us.

The day presented us with a choice. What we wanted was to spend the day having fun but what we needed was to pass our classes to walk across the stage at graduation. We chose the long-term over the short-term. No day at the pool was worth ending up in summer school.

Life presents choices. Each day, wants arise inside our hearts and our minds. Some wants present no danger but far too many have a high price tag for a momentary pleasure. What seems harmless becomes reckless and ends in destruction, but we have a choice.

Paul wrote that the mindset of the flesh is dangerous and ends up in death. The flesh draws us to decide without thought to outcome, pushes us to think of the temporary without thought of the eternal. Irresponsibility emerges from those who only think of "now." What we choose to neglect today can become that which we pay for tomorrow.

"Actions spring not from a thought, but from a readiness for responsibility."

DIETRICH BONHOEFFER

As Christians, we must think long-term. Our minds are set on the glory of God. Paul said that the Spirit leads to life. As we live by the guidance of the Holy Spirit, we choose what we need to do over what we may want to do. By the Spirit's lead, we journey in responsibility rather than languish in immaturity.

Being led by the Spirit is the call for all followers of Jesus. We choose righteousness, even if it means we deny the wants of a day. We set the example by being responsible. Our eyes are set on the long-term rather than being dazzled by the short-term. This season is a chance to mature even more. Maturity comes as we embrace responsibility.

plant the Word—

"For those who live according to the flesh think about the things of the flesh, but those who live according to the Spirit, about the things of the Spirit. For the mind-set of the flesh is death, but the mind-set of the Spirit is life and peace." (Romans 8:5-6, CSB)

pray the Word—

Father, warn us each day of the long-term effect of the choices we make today. Help us to see beyond our own wants and wash clean the mindset of the flesh within us. Give us self-control and perspective. Use the Holy Spirit to guide us to make decisions that bring glory to Your name.

work the Word—

Pray before making decisions. Take a moment to breathe before making those decisions to ensure that you are choosing the path of righteousness, not just reacting. Put on paper the pros and cons of the decision to be made and take enough time to search for any Bible verses that provide extra guidance on the subject.

DID YOU KNOW?

According to Wikipedia, the tradition of skip day traces back to the 1930s. The film *Ferris Bueller's Day Off* gave the tradition more exposure during the 1980s.

"Women weren't created to do everything a man can do. Women were created to do everything a man can't do."

ANONYMOUS

MICHELLE

clothed
IN STRENGTH

EVERY YEAR ON MARCH 8 THE WORLD CELE-
BRATES INTERNATIONAL WOMEN'S DAY. IT'S
A DAY TO CELEBRATE THE GREAT ACHIEVE-
MENTS OF WOMEN AND THE MEANINGFUL
CONTRIBUTIONS THEY'VE MADE TO THE
WORLD.

While there are many contemporary women to
admire, strong and capable women have been
around since biblical times.

Take Esther for example, who stood up to the king
himself, knowing she could be killed for doing so,
because her time had come to save her people.
Or Mary of Nazareth, who braved the stigma of
premarital pregnancy as a teenager, knowing Joseph
might refuse to marry her, because she was called to
give birth to the Son of God. Or Priscilla, who gave up
a simple life to travel and preach the gospel with her
husband Aquilla and the apostle Paul. Or Deborah,
who was a prophet and a judge of Israel (The only
female judge in the Bible). Or Rahab, who put herself
in harm's way by hiding two men who had been sent
to scout out Jericho before attacking the city.

And so many more! Eve, Miriam, Ruth, Mary
Magdalene, Rachel, Hannah, and Sarah—not to
mention all of the unnamed women who obeyed
God, gave everything, and risked it all to accomplish
their purpose in life.

We are also called to be strong, productive women
of faith. And women who are married are also called
to be helpmates to our husbands. These two things
don't have to be at odds. In fact, in Genesis 2:18,
when God said that He would create a woman to
be a "helper" for the man, the original text uses the
Hebrew word "ezer" to mean "helper."

"Ezer" is used in two other contexts throughout the
Old Testament: referring to powerful nations that
Israel sought help from in battle, and again when
referring to seeking God for help.

Being a helper isn't a lowly position; it's an
important one that requires strength!

God designed women and men to complement
each other's strengths and weaknesses. Just check
out Proverbs 31. The passage highlights a woman's
strengths and gives us a great guideline for a happy,
fulfilling life as a woman. Perhaps the most poignant
verse from the chapter is verse 25, NIV: "She is
clothed with strength and dignity; she can laugh at
the days to come."

In an ideal world, every woman would enjoy the
dignity of being a daughter of the Most High God
and the strength of fulfilling her destiny. So be who
God made you to be! Married or unmarried. Stay-at-
home mom or a businesswoman or a combination
of both. Be strong and make no apologies for it.
Sure, International Women's Day is a special day to

honor innovative, strong, difference-making women, but you don't need a holiday to celebrate being the strong, amazing woman that you are every single day. Like Esther, you were created for such a time as this.

plant the Word

"For if you remain silent at this time, relief and deliverance for the Jews will arise from another place, but you and your father's family will perish. And who knows but that you have come to your royal position for such a time as this?" (Esther 4:14, NIV)

pray the Word

Lord, thank You for clothing me in strength and dignity. Embolden me and guide me to use that strength for Your glory. Help me, Lord, to walk in all that You have called me to do. Amen.

work the Word

Read all of Proverbs 31. In a journal, make a list of the attributes you see in the Proverbs 31 woman. How many of them do you think you're walking in right now? What are areas where you can grow?

DID YOU KNOW?
Women statistically have better senses of hearing, smell, and taste than men. Women also see colors and feel textures better than men.

looking for
LUCK AGAIN

ADVENTURE AWAITS IN PATCHES OF GREEN SCATTERED THROUGH THE YARD. A BED OF CLOVER DRAWS OUR ATTENTION AND A SEARCH BEGINS. THE HOPE IS THAT, IN THE MIDDLE OF ALL THAT CLOVER, ONE WITH FOUR LEAVES WILL BE DISCOVERED.

For years, we claimed a patch, whether it be in our front yard or down at Grandma Peggy's house. I always sat on the ground as I rummaged through the section I claimed.

It was imperative to set boundaries. If you didn't, your sister or a cousin could come and try to wade through your clover, only to steal a four-leaf clover from your patch. I wasn't blessed with good luck in life, so I assured that no one came to my clover to steal a symbol of good fortune from me.

"Did you find any?" my cousin asked.

"Nope . . . not so far," I replied, only giving a slight look up to make sure my patch was not being pillaged.

"I found two," he pointed out, showing me his luck with the clover by leaning his hand down to my eye level.

"I've got one," another cousin called out.

As for me, nothing. I couldn't find one. The abundance of clover seemed to blend in. My ADD pulled my thoughts here and there so I likely bypassed one as my mind sifted through random thoughts. Whatever the reason, I failed to pull out the symbolic lucky clover that others seemed to find more easily.

One of the great teachings of the Bible is how to have a blessed life. To be blessed by the Lord does not require us to sit in the grass and sweat under the heat of the sun in the hopes we might find a bit of luck in the process. We can be sure of blessing in this life and beyond by simply reading the Bible and putting into action all that God says leads to blessing.

Our culture is riddled with superstition about luck. The four-leaf clover is but one of many symbols thought to provide an extra push towards the prosperous path of life. Some carry a rabbit's foot while others put stock in a fortune cookie. Some avoid that which supposedly ensures bad luck, like a black cat crossing one's path, walking under a ladder, or breaking a mirror. People want good things to happen to them. They take those steps to ensure the good and avoid the bad.

Thank God we do not have to embark on such a trivial endeavor in life. The Bible guides the way to the blessing of God, by doing things such as taking care of the poor, pursuing the path of righteousness, and being a peacemaker.

"I'm still here, I'm still alive, I'm still blessed, on my way to my destiny, because the favor of God is on my life."

HEZEKIAH WALKER

His blessing isn't limited to a specific clover or a piece of paper inside a cookie. Blessing comes inside God's will and if God says He will bless it, He will surely bless it. There is no luck involved and His favor is more than momentary.

plant the Word—

"Happy is the one who cares for the poor, the Lord will save Him in a day of adversity. The Lord will keep him and preserve him; he will be blessed in the land. You will not give him over to the desires of his enemies." (Psalm 41:1-2, CSB)

pray the Word—

Heavenly Father, thank You for the blessings You pour out in our lives and for teaching us what a blessed life truly looks like. Help us to see how the blessings of our lives can bless others and give us a desire to find blessing through being a blessing. Reveal to us through scripture how to find a life that provides more.

work the Word—

Psalm 41 says that those who take care of the poor will be blessed by the Lord. Look for a local soup kitchen to volunteer at today. Find ministries that focus on the poor and get involved in those ministries. A backpack ministry at our church sends food home with children who have nothing to eat on the weekend, when they cannot receive their school lunch. Start a similar ministry at your church.

DID YOU KNOW?

According to the Guinness Book of World Records, a man named Edward Martin has the largest collection of four-leaf clovers. He has 111,060 in his collection.

"Loving others always costs us something and requires effort. And you have to decide to do it on purpose. You can't wait for a feeling to motivate you."

JOYCE MEYER

MICHELLE

love is better
THAN PANCAKES

MY HUSBAND LOOKS FORWARD TO THE LAWRENCE COUNTY LIONS CLUB SPRING PANCAKE FESTIVAL THAT HAPPENS ON THE FIRST SATURDAY IN MAY EVERY YEAR. ME? NOT SO MUCH.

It's not that I don't love pancakes; it's just that I don't love early Saturday mornings. You see, the Spring Pancake Festival happens very early on that first Saturday in May.

People begin lining up well before 6:00 a.m. in anticipation of a hearty carb-filled breakfast. It's a great place to see most everyone in town because there's always a great turnout for this worthy cause. For years, my sweet mother-in-law, Martha, would pick up Jeff to go with her to the pancake extravaganza, and the two morning birds would have a great time.

It was a wonderful mom/son tradition that I wholeheartedly encouraged. After all, Jeff was able to spend quality time with his mama, and I was able to catch up on some sleep. Our oldest daughter, Abby, began joining her daddy and Nana in this Springtime celebration when she reached middle school age, and a good time was had by all. Jeff, Nana, and

Abby visited and ate pancakes while our youngest daughter, Ally, and I enjoyed a few extra hours of slumber. It was a perfectly wonderful Saturday every year.

But, after Nana passed away in the fall of 2017, I knew the Lions Club Springtime Pancake Breakfast 2018 would be a difficult one for my husband. Nana was such a huge part of our lives, and her absence left a big hole in our family. With both of our daughters married and living elsewhere, Abby was no longer a viable pancake partner for my hubby, so that meant I'd have to step up to the pancake plate. And that's exactly what I did.

Appropriately, it rained that first Pancake Breakfast without Nana. Jeff and I huddled closely under an IU umbrella, remembering Nana, and inhaling the intoxicating aroma of bacon and sausage. It was cold and rainy, but my heart was warm because I knew I was right where I was supposed to be.

Now, I can honestly say I, too, look forward to that first Saturday in May every year—not because I love pancakes, and definitely not because of the early morning wakeup call—but because it brings my husband so much joy. You see, when we took the languages of love test by Gary Chapman,

Jeff's love language was Acts of Service. And, going to the annual Pancake Breakfast is one little act of service I can do that brings a smile to his face, and that makes me happy, too.

When is the last time you did something for someone without any expectations of getting something in return? How long has it been since you went out of your way to be kind to someone? I get it. Life is busy, and it's easy to get wrapped up in your own "stuff," but making time to show the love of God is always worth your while. I once heard my pastor say, "We have to make time to see people the way God sees them and love people the way He loves them. Love is rarely convenient."

Let's make time today to show that unselfish kind of love—no matter what it costs, no matter how inconvenient it is. Just know that a little act of service can make a big impact, and if you're lucky, there might be pancakes involved.

plant the Word—

"Do nothing out of selfish ambition or vain conceit. Rather, in humility value others above yourselves, not looking to your own interests but each of you to the interests of the others." (Philippians 2:3-4, NIV)

pray the Word—

Thank You, God, for loving me with an unconditional kind of love. Help me to love others the same way You love me. And help me to look for ways to be a blessing to those closest to me and to those I encounter outside my little circle. Amen.

work the Word—

It's very helpful to know the different love languages of the people in your family. Why? So you can show them love in a way that will mean the most to them.

If you'd like to learn more about Dr. Gary Chapman's book, *The 5 Love Languages* or if you'd like to take the quiz to see which love language best fits you, go to www.5lovelanguages.com online. It's very enlightening.

DID YOU KNOW?
According to National Geographic, our prehistoric ancestors made their own version of Stone Age pancakes. They made a type of flour out of cattails and ferns and then mixed it with water and baked them on a hot rock. It was a flat cake, made from batter, and fried—a prehistoric pancake.

MICHELLE

memories
OF MAMA

WITH MAY BEING THE MONTH WE CELEBRATE MOTHERS I COULDN'T HELP BUT THINK OF MY LATE MAMA, MARION. MY MOM WAS ALSO BORN IN MAY, AND OFTEN, HER BIRTHDAY AND MOTHER'S DAY WOULD FALL ON THE SAME DATE, AND SHE WOULD ALWAYS TEASE, "I WASN'T BORN A MOTHER SO I EXPECT TWO PRESENTS."

That was my mama. She was funny, feisty, loyal, encouraging, loving, and wise. Even now, over fifteen years since she graduated to Heaven, I think of her daily and reflect on all of the lessons she taught me.

True, she may not have been the best cook in the world (though she could make a mean meatloaf); and she may not have been able to sew on a button to save her life; and she definitely had no sense of direction and spent many hours lost on the backroads of Indiana; but she taught me many valuable life lessons while she was on this earth. And I thought I'd share three of them with you.

*Look for the best in every situation: My Mom was definitely a glass half-full person. No matter what

happened in life, Mom always put a positive spin on it. When given the grim news that her cancer was inoperable, Mom simply said, "Well, doctor, I appreciate all that you've done for me, and I understand that you can't do anything else . . . but it was always in God's hands, and all of my faith is in Him."

And, over the course of her cancer battle, Mom beat many odds and outlived every prognosis the medical experts gave her. In fact, right after the doctor's grim diagnosis, she ordered some cute sandals from QVC, believing she would be going on vacation with us that summer. I loved that about her. Always the optimist. Always walking in faith.

*Be your family's best cheerleader and biggest supporter: My Mama was a constant source of encouragement and support. Looking back on my childhood, I was involved in everything—student council, school plays and musicals, swing choir, dance, drill team, cheerleading, gymnastics, Girls Club basketball and softball, middle school track, Bible quiz team, etc.

Even though I certainly wasn't gifted in all of those activities, I never had a second thought about trying out. You know why? Because my Mom always said, "You can do it!" So, I believed I could . . . and then I did.

She was the same way with my siblings, too, and also with my Dad. Whenever I hear the song, "Wind Beneath My Wings," I immediately think of Mom. She truly was the wind beneath all of our wings, and I am forever grateful. I may not always get it right, but I have tried to be that same wind for my husband and my daughters. A simple, "You can do it!" or a sincere act of service goes a long way. That's a good lesson for all of us.

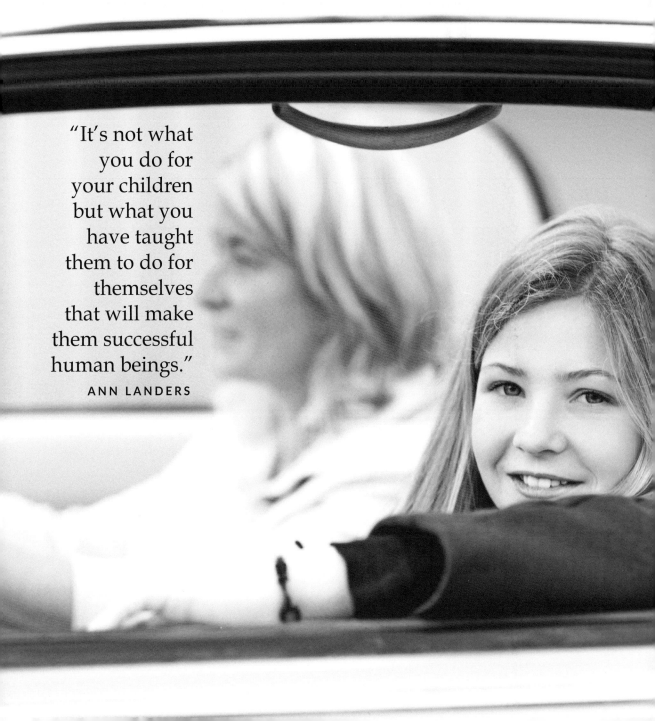

"It's not what you do for your children but what you have taught them to do for themselves that will make them successful human beings."

ANN LANDERS

*Sing loudly . . . even if you don't know the words:
Mom woke up most mornings singing at the top of
her lungs, and she pretty much sang all throughout
the day. She created little ditties for every situation
and occasion, and she often made up her own words
to popular songs. (Or it could be that she just didn't
know the actual words . . . we will never know for
sure.) No matter, Mama sang her way through life
because she chose happiness.

I find myself doing the same thing these days. You'll
often hear me humming to myself or belting out a
chorus or two. In fact, today I was singing along to a
Little Big Town song on the radio: "Why don't we do
a little daydreaming?"

"Mom, it's day DRINKING, not daydreaming," my
youngest daughter informed me, laughing, and
shaking her head.

"Oh," I said. "Well, I like my version better," and I
continued crooning the wrong lyrics.

I am definitely on my way to becoming my mother . . .
and I'm OK with that.

How about you? Do you find yourself becoming
more and more like your mama? If your mother was
a godly woman, then that's wonderful. But maybe
you weren't raised by a Christian mother. Maybe
your mom was abusive. Or maybe you never even
knew your mom! Whatever your situation, you can
still learn from your upbringing. If your parents were
less than ideal, then your lesson is simply, "I can do
better. With God's help, I will do better by my family."

If you harbor anger against your parents —
even if they have already died — choose to
forgive them today.

And, if your sweet mama is still alive, then consider
yourself blessed. Make time for her; celebrate her;
study her; learn from her. Then, someday, you'll be
able to pass on those important lessons to your own
children and grandchildren.

plant the Word—

"Train up a child in the way he should go; even when
he is old he will not depart from it." (Proverbs 22:6,
ESV)

pray the Word—

Thank You, God, for godly mothers. Help me to learn
from my parents, or those who are like parents that
You've put in my life, and help me to honor them.
Amen.

work the Word—

Sometimes, God places "other mothers" in our lives
who care for us and give us needed direction. You
don't have to share DNA with someone to be family,
so why not send a thank-you note to the "other
mothers" in your life? Let them know how important
they are to you.

DID YOU KNOW?
The word "mother" is in the
King James Version of the
Bible 321 times in 293 verses.

"Two roads diverged in a wood, and I— I took the one less traveled by, and that has made all the difference."

ROBERT FROST

ANDY

where does
THE PATH LEAD?

INTO THE WOODS WE GO. SOME TRAILS WE KNOW WELL WHILE THERE ARE OTHERS OF WHICH WE ARE NOT AS FAMILIAR, PATHS NEVER TRAVELED BEFORE. SPRING MAKES US ALL TRAILBLAZERS, TAKING ADVANTAGE OF THE OFFERINGS OF LOCAL PARKS AND THE ADVANTAGEOUS SPIRIT WITHIN US.

One of our favorites leads to a waterfall. After a good rain, the falls are a thing of beauty. The walk is a bit strenuous but once you reach the highlight point, the walk was worth it. Sometimes, though, choosing the wrong path does not end up as well.

"Let's do that one," my girlfriend, who later became my wife, urged as we studied the wooden sign with trail outlines.

"Umm . . . do you see how long that is?" I asked, sure she misread the distance.

"We need exercise," she said, turning to start the trail before I could fully object.

"Uggh . . . " The sound emerged as I knew I had to follow her.

We walked. We walked some more. At one point, she decided we should jog. So, we jogged. The markers for the trail were so bad in places that we actually got lost, wandering around an unkept area until finally rediscovering the trail she chose.

As we finally reached the end, even she regretted the choice of the trail. We saw nothing exciting. We neglected to take water, so we needed something to drink desperately.

I never let her choose a trail again!

As I look back at that day, I see a lesson of life and faith. That Spring stands out because we chose a path that took a lot out of us but left little impact on us, other than a reminder to never go there again. And cramps in the legs that night.

Life presents paths. Every day, people choose the path they will chart. Many assess the requirements of the trails before them and seek to determine the outcome of each option. From a personal set of analytics, a person proceeds in a particular direction in life. Is it the right path? Does the destination match our initial expectation?

The Bible warns that we can be deceived. Appearances draw us down roads we were never intended to take. Blinders lead us to pitfalls. Decisions, opinions, and mindsets dictate what we want to see without allowing for the possibility of derailment.

When choosing a path in life, we need God's guidance. The One who sees what lurks in the future guides us here in the present.

Deciding without consulting Him leaves us in danger of choosing tragedy when He wanted us to experience triumph.

Who guides our day? Who chooses the path for our lives? If we rely only on our knowledge, we will find that the path didn't lead where we thought it would go.

plant the Word—

"There is a way that seems right to a man, but its end is the way to death." (Proverbs 14:12, CSB)

pray the Word—

Heavenly Father, guide us down the path to life, revealing to us the path You designed for our lives. Help us to see as You see and draw our hearts to You before we start out each day. Fill us with Your wisdom today. Thank You for caring enough for us to provide a path for our life that leads to life.

work the Word—

Choose wisely and rely on faith rather than emotion. Emotion leads us into dangerous areas in life. Faith propels us to God, who promises to lead us to life. Use prayer to receive guidance. Absorb direction from the Word. Listen to godly voices and choose the path that promises life.

DID YOU KNOW?

The National Park Service is home to some of the most beautiful trails in the world. In fact, the National Park Service has over eighteen thousand miles of trails.

MICHELLE

can you be ANY LOUDER?

OUR NEWLY SCREENED-IN PORCH PROMISED QUIET, PEACEFUL NIGHTS TOGETHER FOR MY HUSBAND AND ME. AFTER A LONG DAY'S WORK, WE COULDN'T WAIT TO RETREAT TO THE PORCH FOR A FEW MOMENTS OF MOSQUITO-FREE RELAXATION AND CONVERSATION.

The porch was supposed to be a haven, a place to forget what had been, and soak in a few moments of the present peaceful evening. But apparently, our nature friends didn't get that memo.

The comforting hymn of nature, low and peaceful, that greeted us when we plopped down on our porch chairs, soon became like a rock concert, each performer trying to overpower the others.

The bullfrogs hummed their tune, calling out to anyone who would listen. Jealousy sparked the katydids to chime in with a loud song of their own. Unwilling to remain muted, the crickets crept their way in, slowly raising their volume level to match the other performers. As if they'd been cued, the cicadas cried out, offering their unique song, and before

long, all of nature seemed to be fighting to be the dominant decibel in an overcrowded chorus.

It became almost comical.

"It's so pleasant out here, isn't it?" I commented to Jeff.

"What?"

I repeated my sentiment, a bit louder: "I said it's so nice out here, isn't it?"

"What? I can't hear you!"

And so our dreams of quiet conversation and peaceful porch-sitting were not to be. . . .

Croaks of a bullfrog grew louder, drowning out our voices, asserting their dominance, but as they reached a crescendo, the others turned up their volume. Before long, the softness of the moment became a game of "Can you top this?"

Knowing we'd been beaten, we came inside the house and turned on a Hallmark movie.

While that porch performance of "I can be louder than you!" proved quite comical, it's not as funny when we try to "one up" the people we encounter in everyday life. Too many times, a colleague shares about a recent accomplishment, and immediately, you feel the urge to exceed what that person has done. Or someone posts "a humble brag" on social media, and you can't type your "humble brag" fast enough, so you won't be overshadowed. Just as this becomes a nuisance in nature, it is equally annoying in humans.

"Humility is
not thinking
less of yourself,
it's thinking of
yourself less."

RICK WARREN

Life is so much more than a performance, and living a life of "one-upping" everyone else is no way to live.

The measure of a human being is not who can outdo all others on any given task, with the exception of one; serving like Jesus.

The Bible tells us that we are only to outdo one another in showing honor. To show honor is not about putting ourselves on a pedestal. To show honor means to elevate others above ourselves, and to serve wholeheartedly. Our ego pushes us to outdo and outshine others while our faith tells us to walk in humility and shine the light of Christ.

Someone very wise once said, "I can't hear what you're saying because your actions are too loud." Her point was this—our words are often lost because our actions are in total contradiction to the words being spoken. The loudest isn't always the most effective. The greatest, as Jesus said, is the servant, the one who quietly does what needs to be done. If the Son of God can humble Himself enough to wash the feet of others, surely we can stop one-upping the people in our life and instead point them toward Christ. The next time you're on the porch, contemplate how you can better serve others . . . hopefully it won't be so loud that you can't hear your own thoughts.

plant the Word—

"Show family affection to one another with brotherly love. Outdo one another in showing honor." (Romans 12:10, HCSB)

pray the Word—

Father, instill in me a spirit of humility over a spirit of constant competition. Help me to see that one-upping others is more about me than it will ever be about You. Help me to measure my life not by volume but by the validity of who I am in You and by the Word being put into action in my life. Amen.

work the Word—

Take a few moments and reflect on your life . . . where does one-upping occur? When the spirit of competition arises, immediately pray that God would fill that need to be the best, the loudest, and the most important. Ask Him to help you become only who He has called you to be. Be the best you can be in all things but approach it all with the heart of a servant, a heart set on Jesus Christ.

DID YOU KNOW?

An African cicada is the loudest insect in the world. The roar of this cicada registers nearly as loud as a chainsaw.

"Faith is a living
and unshakable
confidence, a belief
in the grace of God
so assured that a
man would die a
thousand deaths
for its sake."

MARTIN LUTHER

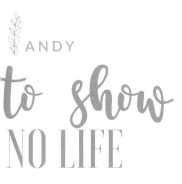

ANDY

to show
NO LIFE

EVERYTHING APPEARS DEAD IN THE WINTER. OTHER THAN THE EVERGREENS, IT'S DIFFICULT TO TELL WHAT CONTINUES TO HOLD LIFE AND WHAT NO LONGER LIVES. BUSHES STAND BARREN. TREES SHARE THE SIMILAR BROWN COLOR OF EXPOSED LIMBS.

Until Spring comes, few signs exist to tell what is dead and what is alive. Most everything looks the same. Yet, with the coming of a new season, signs of life emerge, revealing that which no longer counts as living.

If branches are removed in the winter, even the healthy can be mistakenly removed. As Spring progresses, dead limbs show no sign of life.

"Those need to be taken down," a friend pointed out, his knowledge of trees and landscaping exceeding mine.

"Can you get them?" I asked, not wanting to hire someone else. "Or can we wait on it?"

"Yeah, I can get them. You probably want to get them down now. Those are dead and if you leave them, you're rolling the dice. If a storm comes up, those might come down and damage the roof."

So, the limbs came down. The coming of Spring exposed the danger of the dead among the living. Those limbs posed a threat that had been masked in the winter but revealed in the spring. Their removal meant a storm posed less of a threat.

Each year, Spring leads us to look up, to assess the health of the abundance of trees in our yard. What looked normal in the winter can no longer conceal the truth.

Maybe it's time for a Spring assessment of our faith. Is our faith truly alive or does it simply appear to be alive? Do we have a healthy faith, one that continues to grow, or is it just hanging on but stagnant in its growth, or even dying?

Jesus addressed seven churches in the book of Revelation. Most of the churches had issues they needed to address, with only two avoiding a rebuke. Each was given a chance to change and given a reason to make the change.

Sardis received a criticism that forced them to assess their health. Jesus pointed out the appearance of life, the reputation the church held, but exposed the truth within. He said they were dead, and His assessment is the one that matters. His instructions to the church—strengthen that which has yet to die. They could not live on their reputation anymore. Time showed the withering that was hidden in the past.

Is our faith healthy and vibrant or is it more like the church at Sardis? Are we truly alive?

This season challenges us to live up to the reputation of being a growing disciple of Jesus Christ. Just as Jesus encouraged the church at Sardis to strengthen their faith, we need to heed the words. Let's see what is living and let's grow in Christ, revealing the new life that He gives.

DID YOU KNOW?

The presence of mushrooms and fungal growth is one sign that a tree is dead. Another sign is bark that peels away from the trunk of the tree.

plant the Word—

"I know your works; you have a reputation for being alive, but you are dead. Be alert and strengthen what remains, which is about to die, for I have not found your works complete before My God." (Revelation 3:1-2, CSB)

pray the Word—

Dear Lord, show us where our faith is stagnant or perhaps even dying. Help us to strengthen that which remains so that we may begin growing in You again. Prune this life in this season. Revive that which is on the verge of passing. Let us live up to the reputation and expectation of being alive in Christ.

work the Word—

Look at your faith. Is it growing from week to week? Gauge your growth towards the Lord by looking at last week and comparing it to this week. Are you closer to the Lord this month than you were last month? Plan out a growth pattern in Christ. Find a Bible Study or a devotional to encourage growth. Cut away that which pulls you away from the Lord.

MICHELLE

love is in
THE AIR

MANY POETS HAVE PENNED SONNETS ABOUT SPRINGTIME AND LOVE, BUT AS IT TURNS OUT, SCIENCE BACKS UP THEIR RO-MANTIC WRITINGS. ACCORDING TO BIO-LOGICAL ANTHROPOLOGIST HELEN FISHER, THE BRAIN IS PRIMED TO FALL IN LOVE IN THE SPRING.

She went on to explain in an article published in the *Washington Post* that when light hits the retina in the Spring and goes into the pineal gland, it slows the production of melatonin (which makes people sleepy and less likely to encounter romance.) That's why poets write about the feeling of euphoria and giddiness in the Springtime air—our brains believe it is! Therefore, it is, which makes us ready for romance.

You may be wondering how this scientific proof of love being in the air during the Springtime months directly affects you; here's how. If you're not married, look out! This could be your season when God brings that special someone into your life, and you'll be ready for that "meet cute." Or, if you're already in a relationship, or even if you've been married for thirty years like I have, that feeling of euphoria and giddiness doesn't have to go away just because

you've been with your significant other for a long time, any more than it has to dissipate the day after Spring ends.

Following, are four tips guaranteed to help you keep that loving feeling all year long.

1. ADAPT & ADJUST TO KEEP THE PEACE: What does that mean? That means you shouldn't try to change your spouse. But you say, "My spouse really needs changing." Well, that's not your job—that's God's job. Take your request to God . . . but beware. You know what happened when I used to pray, "Heavenly Father, please change Jeff. He doesn't treat me like he should"? God always showed me how I could treat Jeff better. (Turns out, I'm not perfect . . . and neither are you.)

You can do little things, make minor adjustments, and make a huge difference in your marriage. For instance, if your husband says, "Nothing I do is ever good enough for you." Don't get offended and say, "That's not true and I resent you for saying that." No, realize that your husband is crying out for your approval. Make an adjustment. Put your arms around him and say, "Honey, I am sorry if I've been critical of you. I appreciate everything you do for me and I'm going to try and do better in that area."

Adapt, make adjustments, and keep the peace.

2. STUDY YOUR MATE: Someone once said, "Anything worth having takes work." That's true—especially when it comes to our relationships. You have to work at having a good marriage. It takes effort, but it's so worth it.

We should make it our business to know what our mates like and dislike. Knowing those things will help

"It's spring again. I can hear the birds sing again. See the flowers start to bud. See young people fall in love."

LOU RAWLS

us to work with them and not against them. I try to study Jeff, and then I act on that knowledge. He does the same with me.

For instance, I know if I want to bless Jeff, I will cuddle up next to him on the couch and watch some sci-fi movie involving aliens taking over the world. Am I truly interested? Not really. That's not my favorite genre but I like being with Jeff, and he likes watching intergalactic war movies. In the same way, he watches syrupy-sweet Rom-Coms with me. We show each other honor by doing those things.

So, find out your spouse's likes and dislikes. Study your mate, and act on that knowledge!

3. DO SOMETHING EVERY DAY TO "LOVE ON" YOUR SPOUSE: Pastors and authors Diana and John Hagee call this practice "O.W.E." which is an acronym for: One Way Everyday. O.W.E. prompts them to do something every single day to show each other how much they love one another.

These don't have to be big gestures of love like whisking your mate off to Maui, but don't rule that out. It might be something as simple as sneaking a romantic card into your husband's car that says how much you love and appreciate him. Be creative and have fun with your daily assignment.

Make a conscious decision to make your significant other feel respected, treasured, and adored, and celebrate that springtime-kind-of-love all year long.

4. PRAY FOR YOUR SIGNIFICANT OTHER: Prayer changes things. Spend time each day praying the Word of God over your spouse. Ask your loved one what you should be praying about … any concerns or upcoming work issues that you should be covering in prayer. This will bring you closer. Ever hear the expression, "Those who pray together, stay together"? It's true!

plant the Word—

"Above all, love each other deeply, because love covers over a multitude of sins." (1 Peter 4:8, NIV)

pray the Word—

Father, help me to be the kind of partner that brings honor to You. Help me to love like You love, and Lord, help us to grow closer to You and to each other every single day. In the Mighty Name of Jesus, Amen.

work the Word—

Take this Scripture challenge. Every day for a month, send your significant other a scripture that you're praying over him/her. And, if you don't have a significant other yet, and you desire one, begin praying those same scriptures over the person God has prepared for you.

DID YOU KNOW?
According to Billboard.com the most popular love song of all time is "Endless Love" featuring Diana Ross and Lionel Richie, which stayed at number one for nine weeks in 1981.

"If God is your partner, make your plans big."

D. L. MOODY

ANDY

from one COMES MANY

PACKETS OF SEEDS OFFER A CHANCE AT ABUNDANCE. WITH EACH SEED, THE POSSIBILITY EXISTS THAT PRODUCE WILL COME.

We often buy seed packets from Dollar General or Lowe's. I work the ground and then allow the girls to plant the seed in the holes. We explain what type of seed we are planting as we go.

One of our favorites is green beans. Every member of our little household loves the taste of homegrown green beans. One by one, the seeds fall from little fingers into the hole, then are covered by the soil again.

"Daddy, these seeds just look like a bean. It doesn't look like a plant," Autumn told me one year.

"But a plant will grow out of that bean," I explained, a little too briefly and too abstract according to her reaction.

"Does that mean that when we eat them, a plant will grow out of us?" she asked, her little eyes bulging out at the thought of a plant growing in her little tummy.

"No, honey. It doesn't work like that," I responded, quite amused at her expression and at her understanding of what I said.

We take care of the plants as they emerge and joyously pull from them as they produce. Most of what we choose to plant are high yielding so from one little seed placed in the soil and nurtured comes an abundance of food.

One seed can produce multiple pickings. One pack of seeds can provide for many.

Our lives are like those little bean seeds. Inevitably, some of the seeds never produce anything. Though they are in the same soil, receive the same sunlight and water, nothing comes from them. They fail to produce. Others, though, spring forth out of the soil and what they produce is a blessing. From one comes many.

As Christians, our lives are called to produce fruit. The fruit is to be seen by the world and to bless others. We are called to be disciple makers. Our fruit is that of the Holy Spirit and our one little life is to have an impact on many more lives. God waters and provides; we grow and produce. From such a life, others can experience the goodness of the Lord who longs to be in their lives. He designed us to burst forth and be a blessing in this fallen world.

What is your life producing today? Is there an abundance of fruit or do we need a little holy fertilizer to get us going?

As Spring leads us to the garden, let's think about our existence. Let's look to see who is affected by our faith and what size impact it's having on them. Then, let's pray that God produces even more for His glory, so we feed even more people with what nourishes the soul—Jesus Christ

plant the Word—

"But the ones sown on good ground are those who hear the word, welcome it, and produce a crop: thirty, sixty and 100 times what was sown." (Mark 4:20, CSB)

pray the Word—

Father, thank You for the seed sown in our lives. We pray that you water it and help it to grow. Bring a produce from our lives so that others may come to know You. Help us be disciple-makers. Give us a desire to reach this world and be to a living example of what You can do through a life.

work the Word—

Assess the produce of your life today. If you feel like your life is not producing as it should, get deeper into God's Word and pray. From there, choose a few lives you will pour into from this day forward. Make the time to be invested in their lives.

DID YOU KNOW?
According to PSECU, most tomato plants yield roughly eight pounds of tomatoes per plant.

something to
REALLY CHEER ABOUT

SPRINGTIME BRINGS MANY THINGS—BEAU-TIFUL FLOWERS, WARMER WEATHER, AND . . . CHEERLEADING COMPETITIONS. AS A FORMER HIGH SCHOOL AND COLLEGE CHEERLEADER, THE MOM OF TWO FORMER CHEERLEADERS, AND FINALLY A CHEER-LEADING COACH, I WAS WELL AWARE OF THE IMPORTANCE OF EACH CHEER COMPE-TITION.

What I wasn't aware of was how much this particular one would impact my life.

My oldest daughter Abby and I were loving our new positions as co-coaches of the Shawswick Elementary cheerleaders. They were energetic, lots of fun, and really good! That's why we had been looking so forward to showcasing all of their talent in the countywide competition, and our girls did not disappoint. They nailed their routine, and several of our girls also competed individually for best jumper, best gymnast, and overall best cheerleader.

As the awards presentation began, I whispered to Abby, "I just hope that all of our girls get something—a spirit award—something." She nodded in agreement.

One by one, the awards were presented. We were passed over for best squad, but we did earn an award for the most creative home cheer, as well as a spirit stick for exuding the most school spirit. Also, three of our seven cheerleaders won individual awards—Kennedy won a best jumper award; Ally won a spirit ribbon; and Chelsea earned a best gymnast medal.

As we took pictures of our girls with their group awards and individual merits, I noticed one of our fourth graders, Trista, wasn't as "spirited" as usual. In fact, she seemed quite upset. I was just about to ask what was troubling her, when Chelsea, one of our individual award winners and a fifth grade squad member, put her arm around Trista's shoulder and asked, "What's wrong?"

"I just wish I could've won an award," Trista said, with big tears in her eyes.

Without missing a beat, Chelsea handed Trista the "Best Gymnast" award and said, "You can have this one."

Trista hesitated, not sure if she should accept it, but Chelsea insisted.

"Go ahead," she urged. "It's yours."

Trista hugged Chelsea and then literally bounced away (like Tigger from *Winnie the Pooh*) to show her mom the medal while Abby and I stood there in amazement at the selfless act we'd just witnessed. At that moment, I so wished I'd had an extra-special, ginormous award to give Chelsea for her kind heart.

"Too often we underestimate the power of a touch, a smile, a kind word, a listening ear, an honest compliment, or the smallest act of caring, all of which have the potential to turn a life around."

LEO BUSCAGLIA

I'm not sure if anyone else saw what Chelsea did that afternoon besides Abby and me, but her act of kindness certainly inspired us. Later, I told Chelsea how proud I was of her, and she smiled and sort of brushed it off, not wanting me to make a big deal of it. But it was a big deal. Though Chelsea thought it was just a small gesture, it put a big smile on Trista's face, and it made a huge impression on me. Coaches love that kind of stuff!

And so does God.

I may have taught Chelsea new cheers that year, but she taught me the importance of being kind—even when no one else is looking. She showed me the impact of going the extra mile and truly living out that Golden Rule found in Matthew 7:12.

It's been years since we coached that cheer squad, but I've never forgotten Chelsea's selfless act and the joy it brought to her teammate on that Spring afternoon.

With Spring being all about new life and new beginnings, let's take this season to grow in kindness. Let's be like Chelsea and look for opportunities to emulate Jesus.

plant the Word—

"But the Holy Spirit produces this kind of fruit in our lives: love, joy, peace, patience, kindness, goodness, faithfulness, gentleness, and self-control. There is no law against these things!" (Galatians 5:22-23, NLT)

pray the Word—

Father, help my heart to be sensitive to the needs and hurts of others, and give me the courage to step out of my comfort zone and be Your hands and feet in this world. I love You, Lord. Amen.

work the Word—

Challenge yourself to do one Random Act of Kindness every single day. It can be as small as getting the door for someone to buying someone's lunch in the car behind you at your favorite fast food establishment—just as long as you do something every single day. To keep yourself accountable, why not keep track of those acts of kindness in your journal?

DID YOU KNOW?

In the 1960s, the International Cheerleading Foundation began ranking the best college cheerleading squads. This eventually led to cheer competitions, with the first broadcast of a national college cheerleading competition appearing on CBS in 1978.

"How lavishly our
Father provides!
What bounty!
What abundance!"
CHUCK SWINDOLL

ANDY

the overflow
OF HEAVEN'S WATERS

APRIL SHOWERS NOT ONLY LEAD TO THE BEAUTY OF THE FLOWERS OF MAY, BUT THE POURING RAINS HELP TO CREATE BEAUTIFUL WATERFALLS AROUND THE NATION.

On our ride to the church, an old dam stands just beside the road. The rock creation outlines the north side of Kimesville Lake. During the summer, excess water rarely threatens the dam as intense heat and dry weather keep the level of the lake low.

Below the dam runs a creek that flows through Guilford County. When the rains of Spring fall, the waterfall marks the journey to the church.

"Look out your window girls," I call out to Cheyenne and Autumn.

"Wow, look Autumn," Cheyenne echoes.

"Wow," Autumn comments with a slight glance before returning to a video game or a coloring page.

Every time we go, we take note of the waterfall. Roughly two hundred years old, it once helped power a mill. Now, it powers the faith of my family as we travel past.

The rains from the heavens produce the breathtaking view for all who pass by. Without the provision of Heaven, the waterfall is a dry rock wall with plants growing up the side. But when the rains come, the abundance produces an overflow that cannot be ignored. Many days, caught in the stress of life on this earth, I stop for a few moments just to hear the sounds and feel the spray off the waterfall.

The stunning sight is a direct production of the hands of God in action. He provides and the water overflows.

David understood the waterfall the Lord creates in life. What is dried and parched devoid of the Lord changes drastically in the presence of the Almighty. The 23rd Psalm reveals the heart of someone who has been blessed by God. Through the presence of the Lord, the protection of the Shepherd, and the abundant provisions of the Provider, David's life stood as a waterfall after an abundance of rain.

The shepherd boy turned king proclaimed the overflow of his life. His cup overflowed, the contents of blessing a waterfall that flows beyond what he could hold inside. His response was to be even more immersed in the presence of the One who blesses beyond measure.

If we honestly assess our lives, a waterfall emerges in the recognition of what the Lord has done. Too much time is spent looking at the deficiencies of our lives, focused on what we think we lack. But when we recognize what God has done, we experience a waterfall of biblical proportions, one akin to David's words in Psalm 23.

You have life today. Through Jesus Christ, you have

salvation, hope, forgiveness, and redemption. The sun rises and you have time, moments to share with others and moments to share with the Lord. The beauty of creation surrounds you. Opportunities await you. His word is within reach and His ears are tuned to the cry of your heart. Our cup overflows every day because of the continuous rains of blessing in our lives.

plant the Word

"You prepare a table before me in the presence of my enemies. You anoint my head with oil; my cup overflows. Only goodness and faithful love will pursue me all the days of my life, and I will dwell in the house of the Lord as long as I live." (Psalm 23:5-6, CSB)

pray the Word

Lord, open our eyes to see the waterfall of blessings You pour out in our lives. You give to us so much more than we deserve. Help us to see and appreciate all that we have in You each day.

work the Word

A friend created a visual in her home where she wrote down answered prayers and placed them in a frame. It served as a reminder of God's faithfulness. Write down the blessings in your life. Keep them in a place where you see them daily. Those reminders cascade from us a joy that spreads to others around us.

DID YOU KNOW?

Niagara Falls, possibly the most recognizable waterfall in the United States, is visited by eight million tourists each year.

MICHELLE

spring
CLEANING OF
YOUR SOUL

I DON'T KNOW ABOUT YOU, BUT WHEN SPRINGTIME ROLLS AROUND, MY HOUSE NEEDS A GOOD SPRING CLEANING. ALL OF THOSE CHORES THAT WE PUT OFF—SWEEPING UNDER THE SOFA, DUSTING THE TOP OF THE CABINETS, CLEANING THAT STICKY GOOP OUT OF THE CORNERS OF THE REFRIGERATOR—DESPERATELY NEED OUR ATTENTION.

And that's not to mention all of the clutter that's been building up throughout the year. You know what I'm talking about, right? The stuff you had no idea what to do with, so you shoved it in the closet under the stairs, and now that closet is too full to store your winter clothes and decorations.

Yes, Spring cleaning can be overwhelming. From cleaning to decluttering, it's hard to know where to begin. It might seem like there's an endless list of things to tidy up. But whether you do a full-home sweep in one very intense day or clean a little at a time throughout the season, deep cleaning feels so good when you're all finished. There's suddenly more

room to breathe; your home feels refreshing and peaceful; it's as if you have a fresh start.

That's exactly what Jesus offers us. When you feel like your heart is cluttered or has some sticky goop in the corners, just call on Him and He will come in and deep clean your heart. When you invite Jesus into your life (even the darkest, dingiest corners), He refreshes you and makes you feel peaceful. All you need to do is ask Him to purify your heart; clear out the clutter; and replace that clutter with His love.

I'm not just talking about accepting Jesus as the Lord of your life. That's a great start, but just because we give our hearts to God, that doesn't mean we don't need Him to help us clean up our lives.

Why not spend some time today taking inventory of your life? What are you holding in your heart that is taking up valuable space? What areas could be "cleaned up" a little? Maybe it's a grudge you have against someone. Maybe you're afraid of the future and those worries are dominating your thoughts. Maybe you have become too busy to make time for God. Or maybe it's several of these things. . . .

If you're overwhelmed, make a list of the areas in your heart that could use some spring cleaning. Give your worries to God. Eliminate one distraction at a time. Develop a new godly habit. And pray for guidance as you make improvements. Each week focus on a new area. The Bible says we are attaining from glory to glory, meaning that we are all works in progress. (#progressnotperfection). We may not be perfect, but we are perfectly loved. Be excited about Spring cleaning this year, and let God spruce up your heart and home.

Spring cleaning may have started with the church. Some historians believe that it originated when priests and churchgoers would clean the church leading up to Easter, then would come home and continue the ritual in their houses.

plant the Word—

"Therefore, since we are surrounded by so great a cloud of witnesses, let us also lay aside every weight, and sin which clings so closely, and let us run with endurance the race that is set before us." (Hebrews 12:1, ESV)

pray the Word—

Lord, I ask You to reveal areas of my heart that need some Spring cleaning. Please help me throw out the junk in my heart and fill it with things that are good and pure.

work the Word—

Psalms 139:23, NIV, says, "Search me, God, and know my heart; test me and know my anxious thoughts." Use this verse as a guide to Spring cleaning your life. Ask God to search your heart and point out any hidden grudges or spiritual blind spots you might have. Practice hearing from Him. Learn to be sensitive to the Holy Spirit. And then act on whatever He shows you. It's never easy to tidy up and declutter your life, but it's always worth it.

"Imagine a life with less.
Less stuff, less clutter,
less stress and debt and
discontentment."
RYAN NICODEMUS

"Nobody ever outgrows
Scripture; the book
widens and deepens with
our years."

CHARLES SPURGEON

ANDY

So many STORIES, SO MUCH EXCITEMENT

EVERY SPRING, SCHOOL TRANSFORMED INTO A MASSIVE BOOKSTORE WHICH EXCITED BEYOND MEASURE.

The night before, my mom and dad always gave me five dollars. In the 1980s, five dollars went a long way, especially at the book fair.

"What books are you going to get?" Mom always asked. The question's answer was about as predictable as any other answer of my life.

"Maybe a football book, or a baseball book, or a Charlie Brown book," I'd always tell her as she made sure I put my five dollars in my bookbag.

The next day's adventure highlighted the Spring semester at school. We had an allotted time to browse the books.

My buddy, Eric Fogleman, always scouted the aisles and pointed us to where the sports books were located. We dashed over to find the paperback that told stories of our heroes.

When we found the ones we wanted, we paid our money and returned to class for the rest of the day. The remaining hours dragged by as we eyed the books and watched the clock on the wall. We wanted the school day to end so we could dive deeper into our selections from the book fair.

Some students chose activity books, and some grabbed the latest mystery book. We had friends who picked picture books because of the joy they found in the beauty of the pictures. Some reached for superhero books to read of the triumph of good over evil. I chose sports which told of those who accomplished amazing feats, and I chose Charlie Brown, the guy whose life never seemed to go smoothly but he always ended up better than he started.

Now, decades removed from those days, I still recall the festiveness and excitement. The moments where we read of the incredible and were drawn in with wonder and excitement. What amazing days those were!

Today, we look for much the same. We look for stories of good overcoming evil in a world where evil seems to steadily advance. Our hearts long to hear of incredible feats accomplished by ordinary people. We yearn to hear that the struggles of this life eventually lead to a place where things work out. Incredibly, we don't have to buy multiple books or wait for a book fair to come to town.

The Bible offers more and does so in one edition. The collection of sixty-six books composes a story of love greater than any novel.

People highlighted within the pages are ordinary men and women who, through God, accomplished amazing things. The Bible shows the struggle of so many but the triumph that comes at the end. One book provides more than a thousand books, more excitement than every film released in a decade, and hope that nothing else on Earth can bring.

The book fair made a normal school day a memorable day because of what we found. The same can be said when we open the Bible today and every day. God's Word tells the greatest story ever and we find all we need within.

DID YOU KNOW?

According to Barna's research, one out of five Americans have read the Bible from cover to cover.

plant the Word—

"Princes have persecuted me without cause, but my heart fears only Your word. I rejoice over Your promise like one who finds vast treasure." (Psalm 119:161-162, CSB)

pray the Word—

Dear Lord, give us an excitement to know You more, to grow in our faith. Help us to see how Your Word offers us so much and remind us that the struggle ends in triumph for those who believe in Jesus and accept Him as Savior and Lord. Press us to put down the remote and pick up the Bible every day. Amen.

work the Word—

Spend the time in the Word and it leads us to longing for less time in this world. Find life in the Bible which reconnects us to the Author of Life. Approach the Word with the heart of a child, amazed by the contents and captivated by its truth.

As we set aside a few moments a day, as we dig deeper into the Word, we find that we desire it more. As we see its truth play out in our daily lives, we yearn for more as it prepares us for life.

early morning FISHING

I LOVE TO FISH. I LOVE EVERYTHING ABOUT FISHING EXCEPT FOR ONE THING: GETTING UP EARLY. I'M NOT A MORNING PERSON . . . PERIOD. BUT ANY FISHERMAN WILL TELL YOU THE BEST BITE OF THE DAY IS EARLY MORNING.

Fish are most active around dawn and are more likely to swim near the surface when the hot sun isn't beating down on them. It also helps that there aren't a lot of people around at that time to scare off the fish. As you might expect, this is a huge problem for me, considering I am one of those people who isn't usually out and about before the sun comes up.

I'll tell you this, though. I've never once regretted getting up to go fishing. Not once. Sure, when the alarm clock starts blaring, the last thing I want to do is get out of my warm, cozy bed. But no matter how comfy I am, staying in bed is nothing compared to watching the sun rise over the lake and landing a big ole bass. (Don't worry; we practice catch and release.) I've never come back from a morning of fishing and said, "Man, I wish I'd stayed in bed this morning." I always feel refreshed and accomplished.

You know, I can say the same thing about getting up to spend time with God. When the alarm clock goes off, I know I could hit the snooze button and get a few more minutes of sleep. And once I've woken up a bit, I know I could use that time to get a head start on my work for the day.

It would be much more comfortable to squeeze in some Bible time later in the day once I've had some caffeine. But often, the most comfortable option isn't the most rewarding.

Here's what I've learned. If I don't spend time talking with God first thing in the morning, my whole day is off.

Setting aside that time before I've done anything else is so rewarding, because it sets the tone for my day. During those moments, I ask God to guide my actions before I do anything else. I ask Him to bless my day before it's even begun. And I wait and I listen.

The Bible says that His sheep know His voice, and since I'm a Christian, that means I'm a sheep. Therefore, that means I hear God's voice. So I listen for His voice, that small inward voice, not an audible booming Morgan Freeman voice. Those are sweet times, just being in my Heavenly Father's presence. Those moments are worth getting up for . . . even more than fishing.

So whether you're planning on going fishing or spending time with God, I urge you to stop hitting the snooze button. I know your bed is super comfy, but the rewards you'll reap from this discipline are so much greater.

Seek Him in the morning. It's totally worth it.

"The entire day receives
order and discipline
when it acquires unity.
This unity must be
sought and found
in morning prayer.
The morning prayer
determines the day."

DIETRICH BONHOEFFER

plant the Word—

"You, God, are my God, earnestly I seek you; I thirst for you, my whole being longs for you. . . . " (Psalm 63:1a, NIV)

pray the Word—

Lord, please bless my day today. Guide my steps and lead me in the direction You want me to go. Help me to be more disciplined, and help me to know and hear Your voice above all others. Amen.

work the Word—

Mark 1:35, NIV, says, "Very early in the morning, while it was still dark, Jesus got up, left the house and went off to a solitary place, where he prayed." I always figured if Jesus needed to take time to go off in the morning to spend time with God, then I'm pretty sure I need to do the same. Why not set your alarm and get up earlier tomorrow so you can spend a few moments with God?

DID YOU KNOW?

Fly fishing, the most popular form of fishing, began around the year 200 CE in Mesopotamia.

"We cannot start over, but we can begin now, and make a new beginning."

ZIG ZIGLAR

get your
MOVE ON

SOMETIMES, WE NEED A NEW START IN LIFE IN A NEW PLACE. WE OUTGROW OUR HOME. WHERE WE ONCE LONGED TO BE GIVES WAY TO A NEW DREAM IN A NEW LOCATION.

"What do you think we need to do to put the house on the market," Crystal asked as we prepared to sell our home.

"I don't know . . . I'm not a realtor," I offered as a response, knowing that my expertise is not in anything dealing with a house.

She grabbed a pen and paper.

"Oh geez . . . " I mumbled.

"What?" she said as she scanned the house. "I'm just looking to see what might need to be done."

Two weeks later, a new floor installation crew tore up carpet to lay down laminate. A week after they finished, a new vapor barrier found its way under the house. She decided it was time to move and she was on the move.

If the spirit hits her, there is no time to wait. Truthfully, we had little room and with a new baby on the way, we needed to begin the process of readying the house for an eventual sale.

One professional publication asserted that May is the hot time to move. According to their research and experience, a two-week period in May serves as the most active time for families to uproot from one place and settle in another. The newness of a year gives vision to a new beginning in one's life.

Is it time to make a move in faith? Is this season drawing us to a new location, a nearness to God today? Frozen no more, we have a chance for growth.

James asserts that a move in the right direction is a move that leads to fulfillment. He assured the reader that if we draw near to God, He draws near to us. With every step we make towards Him, He pulls closer to us. He wants us to be near Him. He longs for us to find our eternal dwelling place in Him.

Psalms talks repeatedly about the Lord being our refuge, or dwelling place, in life. Too often, we fail to see the Lord as such.

A new season's here. A new chapter can be written starting today. No matter where you have been in relationship with the Lord before, today offers us the chance to make a move. Find the excitement of what can be in Him. Run to the place the soul calls home. See Him as your refuge and move closer today.

plant the Word—

"Draw near to God, and He will draw near to you. Cleanse your hands, sinners, and purify your hearts, you double-minded people!" (James 4:8, CSB)

pray the Word—

Lord, we want to grow closer to You this Spring. Help us to be on the move towards You throughout this season and beyond. We long to move from where we have been to be closer to You every day.

work the Word—

Make a plan. How can you grow closer to the Lord, or draw nearer, in your personal life? What steps can you take to draw nearer to God with your family? How can you draw even closer to God with your church family? Just as we make a plan before we move into a new home, we need a plan to be able to move closer to God in life.

DID YOU KNOW?

According to Business Insider, the worst time to sell your house is in October and in December.

MICHELLE

metamorphosis

WHILE I WAS FILLING UP THE BIRD FEEDERS TODAY, A BEAUTIFUL YELLOW BUTTERFLY ZIPPED RIGHT OVER MY HEAD. I STOPPED WHAT I WAS DOING FOR A MOMENT JUST TO ADMIRE IT. GOD CAME UP WITH SOMETHING REALLY BEAUTIFUL WHEN HE CREATED BUTTERFLIES!

As I watched that lovely yellow butterfly flit from one flower to another, it was hard to imagine that just a short while ago, that beautiful creation was a very ordinary caterpillar. Talk about a transformation!

You know, God does the same thing for us. Even though we are imperfect, and our hearts aren't all that impressive, when we choose to live for Christ, God transforms us into something new and better than ever. He completely changes our lives and our hearts. And when we mess up or make a wrong turn, He is willing to forgive us over and over again.

Maybe you don't feel beautiful and new like a butterfly right now, but that's okay. You may still be in the transformation process. Caterpillars don't change into a beautiful butterfly overnight.

Did you know that a caterpillar doesn't just grow wings to become a butterfly? When it creates its chrysalis, it actually completely deconstructs inside. Its whole body comes apart, then rebuilds into a completely new creature: the butterfly. It's a rather messy process. Why would we think our transformation would be any faster or any less messy?

The moment we give our hearts to God and ask Him to forgive us of our sins and take control of our lives, the Bible says we become a new creature in Christ Jesus.

That's instantaneous but the process of changing into a beautiful butterfly might take a bit longer. Our old habits. Our old way of life. Those things might take longer to shake off as we attain from glory to glory. (2 Corinthians 3:18)

God is continually deconstructing our old selves and building us into something new. The process can be a messy one, just like the process of a caterpillar turning into a butterfly, but the result is magnificent!

"We delight in the beauty
of the butterfly, but rarely
admit the changes it has
gone through to achieve
that beauty."

MAYA ANGELOU

plant the Word—

"Therefore, if anyone is in Christ, the new creation has come: The old has gone, the new is here!" (2 Corinthians 5:17, NIV)

pray the Word—

Lord, I give my life to You. I ask You to transform me into a new creation, more pure and lovely than ever before so that I can fulfill my destiny here on earth. I love You. Amen.

work the Word—

In your journal, create a list of ways you have been made new since you gave your life to Christ. It's important that we don't beat ourselves up for not being perfect. We'll never be perfect until we get to Heaven, but we can celebrate the little changes—the little victories—along the way.

DID YOU KNOW?
Some butterflies can taste with their feet to test whether a leaf is good to eat.

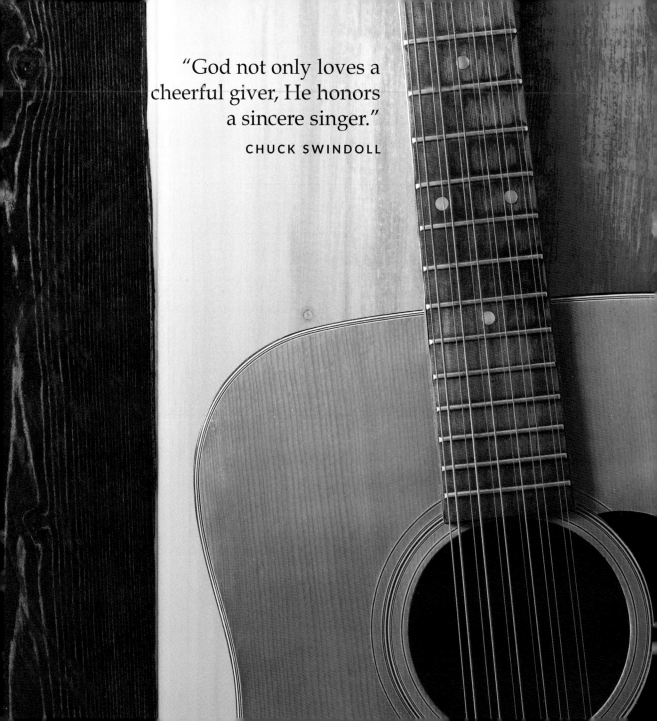

"God not only loves a
cheerful giver, He honors
a sincere singer."

CHUCK SWINDOLL

ANDY

a spring day...
AND RONNIE MILSAP

EVERY SPRING, CROWDS DESCENDED TO GRAHAM, NORTH CAROLINA, FOR A FESTIVAL CALLED ARTS AROUND THE SQUARE.

Lines of crafts and food trucks transformed the area near the Graham courthouse. People strolled around, absorbing the warmth of the day and the joy of an outdoor festival. The staple of Spring beckoned us to embrace a once-a-year celebration. One particular year stood out above all others.

Festival organizers outdid themselves as they attracted Ronnie Milsap to perform. His story amazed me as the country singer overcame so many obstacles to achieve his dream. When his name appeared in the local paper, I had to go.

"I don't even like country music," my friend, Daryl, said as I called him to go. "You know that I hate country music."

"But it's Ronnie Milsap," I explained.

He paused. He didn't want to go.

"Come on, man," I implored. "It'll be fun."

Being the friend he was, he gave in and went with me.

We saw a few others from our high school, stopping to talk as I anxiously awaited the moment Ronnie Milsap took to the makeshift stage.

Finally, the moment came. He sat at the piano and began to sing.

When the time came for "Smoky Mountain Rain" to be sung, hundreds joined in as the sound filled the air. A song rose from those out enjoying the beauty of a Spring day and the festivities in a small town in North Carolina.

The coming of Spring gives birth to a new song in our lives. Sounds of hope rise from lips once silenced by winter's cold. A song of life begins as nature shows signs of new life. From the depths of the soul, a chorus billows each year as life sprouts from within.

Psalm 96 calls for a new song to be sung to the Lord. The song is one of worship and praise in recognition of the splendor of the Lord. As the song of Spring arises from hearts of joy, the song is to be heard by all people. A chorus of the glory of God should rise so that the whole world hears the tune of our hearts in recognition of God's majesty.

A world notices the beauty of Spring. But do they know Who is the artist whose work is on display?

Our voices come together to acknowledge the hand of God as He dresses a once bland world with the beauty only He can bring. Psalm 96 implores us to sing a new song and declare His works among all the people. As we sing this song unto the Lord among the people, they are amazed not only by creation, but are drawn to the Creator.

Amazed by Him, caught up in the beauty of the moment, a song flows from our soul as He has brought forth the signs of life. We sing in triumph. We shout in amazement. We acknowledge Him and declare to the world that our God is the melody of our soul as He orchestrates the rebirth of all that once appeared lifeless.

DID YOU KNOW?

The Bible speaks of singing over four hundred times. According to *Desiring God*, there are fifty commands to sing in Scripture.

plant the Word—

"Sing to Yahweh, praise His name; proclaim His salvation from day to day. Declare His glory among the nations, His wonderful works among all peoples." (Psalm 96:2-3, CSB)

pray the Word—

Lord, let the song of our lives be one of worship to Your name. May we sing of Your glory to all people that they may look to the Source of the beauty of Spring.

work the Word—

Sing a song of praise today! As others speak of the beauty of creation, point them to the beauty and creativity of the Creator. Spring offers us a chance to sing of the majesty of God as His presence is witnessed all around us. People see the effect of the season giving us the chance to sing of the Creator of the season.

MICHELLE

finding JOY

WHEN JEFF ANNOUNCED THAT WE WOULD HAVE TO CUT DOWN THE OAK TREE— THE ONLY BIG TREE— IN OUR BACKYARD, I BEGGED HIM TO LEAVE IT ALONE. SURE, IT WAS COMPLETELY HOLLOW AND DYING FROM THE INSIDE OUT, BUT I JUST COULDN'T STAND TO SEE IT COME DOWN.

I fed the birds from that tree. It provided shade when I read outside. It was the focal point of our backyard. It was one of my happy places, and I couldn't imagine it being gone.

I was dreading the day the tree would come down. As the workers pulled into our driveway that morning, I pleaded once again with my husband to let the tree remain a while longer. But it wasn't to be. Jeff explained the tree had to come down because it had become a danger.

"The next big storm could send the massive tree into our house," he said.

I understood his reasoning, but I hated it just the same. I knew I was going to miss that wonderful tree.

As the men began removing the old Oak, I was prepared to shed a few tears. What I was not prepared for was a sweet surprise. As the workers carefully lifted a large section of the tree, we discovered a mama racoon and her babies. They were so cute! Right away, we called the Indiana Wildlife (DNR) relocator, who carefully transported them to a safer home. All the while, we got to enjoy the adorable raccoon family right in our own backyard.

What I thought would be an awful day turned into a sweet memory. I learned a lesson that afternoon: even less-than-ideal circumstances can contain unexpected moments of joy. Since then, I've tried to find joy in the midst of chaos. It's sort of like finding that silver lining, you know? God always has surprises for us, big and small, if we'll just take time to notice.

Maybe you're in a similar situation: things aren't panning out the way you'd hoped, and it feels like everything in your life is spiraling out of control. I challenge you to look for little things to find joy in amidst the disappointment and craziness. And if you just can't see any joy today, just meditate on His goodness. There is always something to take joy in—I promise! Don't believe me? The Apostle Paul backs me up on this one.

In Paul's letter to the church at Philippi, he mentions "joy" or "rejoicing" sixteen times. What makes that so amazing is this—Paul was in prison when he wrote Philippians. And, it wasn't just any prison, according to Greek scholar Rick Renner of Renner Ministries. It seems this Roman prison was known as one of the worst prisons in the entire country. It had actually been used as a septic hole for many years and had evolved into a prison for the worst offenders.

"It is this broken road with pitfalls and sharp turns and unexpected traverses that has brought me joy and adventure."

ALICE WALKER

Prisoners were chained with their arms above their heads and forced to stand waist-deep in human waste. The prisoners had to stand at all times—no matter how weary they grew. And the smell was so horrid, many prisoners died from the toxic fumes alone! Others died from rat bites and infection. Still, others died from hopelessness. It was that bad—so awful it sucked the very life right out of many strong men.

The prison was dark all day and all night except for the few moments of limited light when the guard fed the prisoners. There were no windows. No ventilation. No reason for joy. So, how could Paul write about rejoicing in the Lord?

Paul learned that the source of his joy had nothing to do with his environment or his physical state. He found joy in Jesus Christ. That's why Paul was able to write: "Rejoice in the Lord always. I will say it again: Rejoice!"

Paul was surrounded by dung and darkness, but his heart was full of joy and Jesus. He fixed his eyes on eternal things. If Paul could still find a reason to rejoice during those dark days, then so can we! Search for the silver lining in those storm clouds—or adorable racoons in a tree trunk!

Look for reasons to praise God, because He wants to surprise you with a special dose of joy. And, if you can't find even one thing to be joyful about today, simply meditate on the Lord and all His promises. That's sure to give you a joy boost.

plant the Word

"May the God of hope fill you with all joy and peace as you trust in him, so that you may overflow with hope by the power of the Holy Spirit." (Romans 15:13, NIV)

pray the Word

Lord, help me to notice the big and little things that bring joy. And help me to focus on You and Your promises in the midst of disappointing situations. I love You. Amen.

work the Word

In your journal, write a list of ten joys you've discovered recently, despite—or maybe because of—your current circumstances.

DID YOU KNOW?

Our brains are hardwired to not notice good things that happen, so it requires extra effort to find them in our day-to-day lives.

"Thriving churches have the Great Commission as the centerpiece of their vision, while dying churches have forgotten the clear command of Christ."

THOM RAINER

ANDY

runners OF FAITH

STRAWBERRY PLANTS MAKE SPRING A SEASON TO LOOK FORWARD TO EACH YEAR. THE BEAUTY OF A STRAWBERRY FIELD EXCITES THE SOUL OF THOSE YOUNG AND OLD.

When I was a young boy, my mother bought me some strawberry plants so I could have my own little strawberry patch at home. After that first year, I noticed the plants growing larger and shoots emerging from the plants we put in the ground a year prior.

"What are those?" I asked, knowing nothing about the plants, primarily focused on the result of the plant above all else.

"Those are runners. It's like a baby strawberry plant," my mom explained as she knelt down to work the soil and the plants.

She spent time learning about the ins and outs of strawberries, so I knew she knew what she was talking about.

"So, what do you do with them?"

"You can replant them. Then, you'll have more strawberry plants."

My excitement grew as I dreamed of an ever-expanding patch in our backyard. What began with twenty plants could grow to hundreds over the years.

We diligently worked the patch for years and watched it expand. Each year, we saw and enjoyed the growth. There was a lot of work involved but the payoff was worth it. Each year's growth fueled a passion for what the next year might bring.

Just as Spring offers the opportunity to expand the goodness of a strawberry patch, this season and this day offers us a chance to expand something even greater — the kingdom of Heaven.

We have the chance to advance the gospel in this season so others can enjoy the sweetness of salvation for themselves.

Jesus gave clear instructions for His followers before He ascended into Heaven. His disciples learned from Him for three years, now He sent them out. Their call was to make disciples, to pour into the lives of others in such a way that the kingdom expanded. He pointed them to grow runners of faith, to be the plant and produce the offshoots. And they did. They took the gospel out and touched the lives of thousands for Jesus Christ.

The Great Commission revealed the work of the gospel in the lives of true disciples. A disciple embraces the gospel, grows in the Word, then sets out to expand the kingdom every day. Jesus told them to do what He did. He called them, taught them, and from Him, they produced fruit. Now, they needed to do the same.

Those words from Jesus echo to us today. Our lives must produce fruit and as disciples, we produce more disciples. As we do, a small group becomes a larger patch, each one producing more runners of faith. The goodness of the gospel spreads and the kingdom advances. Let's work on producing runners this season!

plant the Word —

"Go, therefore, and make disciples of all nations, baptizing them in the name of the Father and of the Son and of the Holy Spirit, teaching them to observe everything I have commanded you. And remember, I am with you always, to the end of the age." (Matthew 28:19-20, CSB)

pray the Word —

Father, give us a heart to reach more people. Take us to the place where we can no longer sit still, but are propelled forward for the sake of the gospel.

work the Word —

Many people struggle with sharing their faith. Start by simply opening up your table to a meal with a few friends who are unbelievers or even young believers. Begin with life and let the Lord open the doors to share your faith. Start a group that centers around a hobby and begin to add faith into the conversations.

DID YOU KNOW?

A single strawberry plant can form between thirty and fifty runners.

MICHELLE

stormy WEATHER

HERE IN INDIANA, WE GET HUGE STORMS IN THE SPRINGTIME. I ACTUALLY FIND MYSELF ENJOYING THE SOUNDS OF RAIN AND THUNDER ON A COOL SPRING NIGHT. BUT OUR DACHSHUND MILLER WAS NEVER SO FOND OF THEM.

Even if we didn't know the forecast, Miller knew. It was like his doggie superpower. I often thought we should've rented him out to our local meteorologists who were not nearly as accurate as good old Miller.

Before the sky ever turned gray or the first raindrop formed, Miller was already shaking, slobbering, and whining because he could sense the storm was coming, and he was already anticipating the thunder and lightning. Miller was terrified of storms. We had no idea how to console poor Miller. Nothing we tried seemed to help.

Finally, we decided to order Miller a thunder jacket on the recommendation of our veterinarian. The thunder jacket, our vet explained, is a weighted coat for dogs that applies pressure to their torso, giving them the same feeling as a hug or a baby swaddle. The pressure is supposed to calm and comfort the petrified pooches. We weren't sure if it would help Miller, but we'd already tried everything else, so we ordered one. The next time Miller started slobbering, shaking, and whining, I grabbed the thunder jacket and put it on him, and just like that, he calmed down. No more slobbering. No more shaking. No more whining. Just one docile dachshund.

You may not be anxious when an actual storm is blowing in, but what about when the storms of life threaten? When you sense that something bad might happen, do you let that fear eat away at you? Do you worry endlessly over all of the "what if" scenarios?

It's easy to let anxiety overtake our daily lives and hold us captive to fear. It can literally incapacitate us, just like Miller's fear of storms controlled his life every time the thunder rolled.

Maybe you're going through a very real storm in your life right now, and you're wishing you had an adult-sized thunder jacket to put on. Well, I can't make that wish come true, but I have good news. You don't need a thunder jacket to ease your fears and get you through this storm, because you have a Heavenly Father who promises to never leave you or forsake you. He will comfort you and give you His supernatural peace. Just remembering that He is right there, holding you, and loving you should give you a secure feeling. Way better than a thunder jacket.

"God's peace is not the calm after the storm. It's the steadfastness during it."

DR. MICHELLE BENGSTON

plant the Word—

"Suddenly a furious storm came up on the lake, so that the waves swept over The boat. But Jesus was sleeping. The disciples went and woke him, saying, 'Lord, save us! We're going to drown!'

"He replied, 'You of little faith, why are you so afraid?' Then he got up and rebuked the winds and the waves, and it was completely calm.

"The men were amazed and asked, 'What kind of man is this? Even the winds and the waves obey him!'" (Matthew 8:24–27, NIV)

pray the Word—

God, I ask You to hold me right now. Comfort me in my time of need. Calm my spirit and give me Your supernatural peace. Amen.

work the Word—

Just knowing what the Word says about a topic can make you feel more secure in life and in God.

*Isaiah 41:10, NIV, says, "So do not fear, for I am with you; do not be dismayed, for I am your God. I will strengthen you and help you; I will uphold you with my righteous right hand."

*Deuteronomy 31:6, NIV, says, "Be strong and courageous. Do not be afraid or terrified because of them, for the Lord your God goes with you; he will never leave you nor forsake you."

*Psalms 121:7, NIV, says, "The Lord will keep you from all harm--he will watch over your life; the Lord will watch over your coming and going both now and forevermore."

DID YOU KNOW?

About sixteen million thunderstorms happen worldwide every year according to NASA.

> "When I stand before God at the end of my life, I would hope that I would not have a single bit of talent left but I could say I've used everything you gave me."
>
> ERMA BOMBECK

a producing
PATCH

THOUGH THEY CAN BE FOUND AT OTHER TIMES IN THE GROCERY STORE, NOTHING COMPARES TO THE FRESHNESS AND JOY OF STRAWBERRIES PLUCKED STRAIGHT OUT OF A FIELD.

What some consider to be work is to others a great family outing. All winter, there is a longing for a day out in the middle of strawberry plants, ones loaded with ripened fruit.

As Spring progresses, we watch the pages of local strawberry farms to see when the berries are ready to be picked. Once they open, we drive out to spend a few hours pulling the perfect strawberries.

Row after row of vibrant green plants catch our eyes as we pull into the dirt parking lot. The sun provides warmth in the morning but becomes oppressive in the afternoon, so an early excursion makes for a more enjoyable experience.

For a couple hours, we fill up quart containers. My wife plans to make a pie and the children beg to eat a quart when we arrive home.

"Can we take some to Grammy and Kyndall?" the girls ask.

"Absolutely. We need to make sure we send them the good ones," we explain to the girls.

The girls, eager to fill containers, are known to pick some that aren't quite ripe and some that look great on one side but are mushy on the other.

For a week, we enjoy the fruits of our labor and seek to bless others with what we picked. Amazingly, a couple hours investment brings a blessing for days. When we run out, we make our way again to the fields to replenish the refrigerator and give out to others.

The Spring provides this opportunity. We teach of the benefits of working, we spend time making memories, and we seek to be a blessing to others with the produce. A beautiful season is marked by these beautiful opportunities.

A day in the field ends with the joy of the harvest. One of our favorites is angel food cake, strawberries, and whipped cream.

Paul encouraged the Corinthian church. His words were meant to keep them focused on what they needed to do each day until the Lord comes again, or they met Him face to face. The apostle told the church that their efforts were not in vain. What they were doing in the name of the Lord was anything but a waste of time.

The toil of labor today led to a reward later. For the Corinthians, the payoff was pleasing the Lord and the effect their efforts had on the lives of others in their city. The sweetness of pleasing the Lord kept the people laboring even when it seemed like the efforts were barely drops in a bottomless bucket.

Sometimes, our efforts feel the same. What seems small and perhaps unproductive at the moment will lead to an amazing reward later, if we continue on, excelling in what we are called to do. The sweat of this moment will lead to something sweet a little while later.

plant the Word—

"Therefore, my dear brothers, be steadfast, immovable, always excelling in the Lord's work, knowing that your labor in the Lord is not in vain." (1 Corinthians 15:58, CSB)

pray the Word—

Heavenly Father, remind us that what we do in Your name is never a waste of time. The work You've called us to is a blessing to our soul and will produce the sweetness of satisfaction over time.

work the Word—

No other effort in life promises more than can effort for the Lord. Sweat always precedes the sweetness of the harvest. The work may seem slow at times but keep going. The payoff is always worth the investment. Dig in today for the Lord, putting forth the best of what you've got toward what the Lord is calling you to do.

DID YOU KNOW?
In 2019, 1.2 million tons of strawberries were produced in the United States.

MICHELLE

seasonal CHANGES

IN THE WINTER, IT'S SO EASY TO WISH THE SNOW WOULD MELT AND MAKE ROOM FOR SPRING. FINALLY, SPRING COMES, AND WE'RE HAPPY FOR A LITTLE BIT. BUT THEN IT GETS RAINY FOR DAYS ON END, AND THEN OUR ALLERGIES START ACTING UP, AND WE FIND OURSELVES WISHING AWAY SPRING IN FAVOR OF SUMMER.

On and on the cycle goes, until we've spent an entire year just wishing for a different season. If we're not careful, we'll end up wishing our lives away.

There's a blessing and a burden for every season. This is true for seasons of the year as well as for seasons of life. Instead of focusing on the burden, why not focus on the blessing?

Yes, Springtime brings allergies, but without the allergenic pollen, we wouldn't have the beautiful flowers that also come with springtime. Focus on the flowers, not the allergies.

If you spend months just longing for the warmer days of Summer, you'll miss out on enjoying those cool breezes of Spring. Every season holds both good and not-so-good things. For instance, I love Springtime fishing. That's when the fish are biting . . . but so are the bugs! All of the bugs come back in full force, and that's a part of Spring I could do without.

Whenever I complain about the bugs buzzing me, my husband will always tease, "Honey, it's all a part of the experience." While I hate to admit it, he's right! You take the good with the bad. That's life. It's all a part of the experience, and I don't want to miss one moment of this great life longing for something else.

Maybe you're in the middle of a life season that you feel like you're just "waiting out," just trying to hold on until the next season, a better season, comes along.

In a few years, you may not be experiencing the same burdens you are facing now, but I can promise you there will be new ones because as long as we're this side of Heaven, we will encounter trouble (John 16:33).

And you may even find yourself missing the joys that you have available to you right now, in this season. So, stop wishing your life away and start enjoying all of the good things today has to offer. Let's not waste our lives always looking for the next best thing. Let's live in the present and find joy in it.

plant the Word—

"My times are in your hands; deliver me from the hands of my enemies, from those who pursue me." (Psalm 31:15, NIV)

pray the Word—

Lord, I thank You for this season of my life. I'm carrying many burdens, but I entrust them to You so I can focus on Your blessings instead. Help me, God, to live in the present and enjoy today. Thank You for every season of life. Amen.

work the Word—

In your journal, make two lists: one list of the burdens in this season of your life, and one list of the blessings in this season of your life. Spend time praying over the burden list, trusting God to carry you through each challenge. Then, spend time praising Him for your blessings list.

DID YOU KNOW?

Earth has season changes because it is tilted about 23.5 degrees.

"Each moment
of the year
has its own
beauty."

RALPH WALDO EMERSON

"The best remedy for those who are afraid, lonely, or unhappy is to go outside, somewhere where they can be quiet, alone with the heavens, nature and God."

ANNE FRANK

ANDY

a blanket,
A BRUNCH,
AND A BLESSING

BESIDE A LOCAL LAKE OR OUT IN AN OPEN FIELD, AN OPPORTUNITY AWAITS. AS SPRING OFFERS US WARMER TEMPERATURES AND BEAUTIFUL GREEN GRASS, WE HAVE THE CHANCE TO STEP OUTSIDE, SLIDE AWAY FROM THE TABLE, AND SUPPLEMENT A MEAL WITH THE BEAUTY OF CREATION.

One of the best spring activities is to have a picnic, to enjoy some time with friends or family. No devices needed. Noisy restaurants avoided. A blanket, some brunch (or lunch), and a blessing of time.

Our family looks for new places to enjoy a remote meal. One year, we laid out a blanket on the shore of Lake Mackintosh for a brunch. Another time, we chose Cedarock Park and set up near the waterfall. The roar of the falls provided a natural soundtrack for the meal. Last year, we packed up and headed to Old Salem, a historical Moravian village.

A breeze keeps the heat from taking over.

A blanket serves as a table.

A brunch becomes a blessing.

For a moment, the contents of the meal matter little. The company makes the event a special time. I refuse to answer my phone. We tune in to each other and the sounds nature provides.

We laugh a lot. Our kids point out different aspects of what surrounds them. The setting is not a bustling restaurant and the cuisine is not prepared by a five-star chef. Those things do not matter.

For a moment, we consume ourselves with the greatness of God. What He provides, we enjoy and we rejoice that we have these moments. Life is good because God is good.

David understood the greatness of God. His personal relationship, the nearness he had to God, catches the attention of all who read Psalm 23. God is not distant to David. David speaks of God as his all in all, proclaiming that the Shepherd provides all he needs. David needed to search for nothing else because what God offers fulfilled.

David further elaborated. The Shepherd took him to the place where his soul was fed. The serenity of David's words flood from the page. The Lord allowed him to lay down in fields of beautiful grass. The lushness of the area added a richness to his relationship with the Lord. The pastures appear through the guidance of the Shepherd. To lie down points to the greatness of God who allows us to rest in a place of beauty, to unwind in the serenc.

The green pastures surround us today, but we are often too distracted to see. A pasture, a field, a grassy patch beside the pond begs us to stop running and find a momentary blessing for the day. We make the time to eat. Sometimes we just need a different location to remind us of the provision of the Shepherd.

plant the Word

"He lets me lie down in green pastures; He leads me beside quiet waters." (Psalm 23:2, CSB)

pray the Word

Heavenly Father, help me find rest in the pastures You provide in my life. Draw my eyes to those places where You calm my soul and help me to rest in Your presence. Thank You for providing for my life and for the rest only You can provide.

work the Word

Open your eyes to see the possibility to find rest around you. Trade in a fine dining experience to enjoy a meal away from the chaos. Take the time to take a break and identify where a picnic can help you reconnect with others as you disconnect from the world. Unwind in the serenity of a place where you are surrounded by God's goodness.

MICHELLE

be the
PINK SHELL

SPRING BREAK IS A YEARLY HIGHLIGHT FOR MANY FAMILIES. IT'S A WEEK TO TRAVEL TO BEAUTIFUL LOCATIONS, TAKE A BREAK FROM WORK AND SCHOOL, AND SIMPLY BE TOGETHER. WHETHER DOING A "STAYCATION" OR HITTING THE ROAD FOR A FAMILY ADVENTURE, I'VE ALWAYS LOVED SPRING BREAK.

One year, our family visited St. Pete Beach, and I absolutely loved getting up early each day to walk the quiet stretch of beach before hundreds of fellow vacationers planted themselves on the lovely white sand. (Though I'm not much of a morning person, this peaceful time only happened in the early morning hours, so I morphed into a morning person for that one week.)

One morning as I walked along the shoreline, listening to the waves and the seagulls, I noticed many more shells on the beach than the previous days I'd walked. They were so numerous, in fact, that I had to slip on my shoes because it was painful to step on them. There were beige and white and gray-colored shells for as far as I could see. Then, several feet away, smack dab in the middle of the neutral-colored shells, a pretty pink one glistened in the morning sun. Of course, my eyes went right to the pink shell because it stood out.

Anytime we go to the beach, I always choose one shell to bring home as a souvenir of sorts, and I knew I'd found the perfect choice. That pink shell now sits on a shelf in my office as a reminder—"In a sea of beige shells, be a pink one."

When it comes to life, we're often afraid to stand out from the crowd. We worry that being different will mark us as someone to stay away from—it's just safer to blend in, isn't it? But when I saw the pink shell that was different from all the rest, I was drawn to it. I wanted to look at it more closely. Its brightness made me appreciate it all the more.

As Christians, we are supposed to stand out. We have been transformed by God's love, so it's only natural we would be different than those who haven't yet encountered Him. Just as that pink shell shone brightly in the sun that morning on the beach, we are to shine brightly for Jesus in a world that's often dark.

When people look at us, they should want to know what makes us different. Upon closer inspection, they should see we have strong values, love without limits, a generous spirit, and an unshakable hope for the future.

Sure, some may think it's weird, but most will be drawn to those Christlike qualities. And if they ask, you can tell them you are different because you have the Holy Spirit within you. Don't be afraid to stand out and be the unique person God created you to be. The perfect Creator created you exactly the way you are for a reason. Embrace that gift from God! Be the pink shell.

plant the Word—

"Do not conform to the pattern of this world, but be transformed by the renewing of your mind. Then you will be able to test and approve what God's will is— his good, pleasing, and perfect will." (Romans 12:2, NIV)

pray the Word—

God, I thank You for the way You created me. Fill me with Your Spirit so that those around me can see how I have been transformed by You. Amen.

work the Word—

Why not go on a nature walk this week and look for things that stand out? Write about it in your journal. And maybe meditate on these scriptures about standing out for the Lord:

Philippians 2:15, ESV, says, "That you may be blameless and innocent, children of God without blemish in the midst of a crooked and twisted generation, among whom you shine as lights in the world."

1 Peter 2:9, ESV, says, "But you are a chosen race, a royal priesthood, a holy nation, a people for his own possession, that you may proclaim the excellencies of him who called you out of darkness into his marvelous light."

DID YOU KNOW?

Just like snowflakes or fingerprints, no two seashells are identical.

"What sets you apart can sometimes feel like a burden and it's not. And a lot of the time, it's what makes you great."

EMMA STONE

"It's time to let God's love cover all things in your life. All secrets. All hurts. All hours of evil, minutes of worry."

MAX LUCADO

ANDY

those nights
ON THE PORCH

TOO COLD FOR COMFORT DURING THE WINTER MONTHS, SPRING OPENS THE DOOR FOR NEW AREAS OF THE HOUSE TO BE ENJOYED.

Out come the rocking chairs that were stored away when winter arrived. Each rocking chair adds to the front porch and beckons us to stop running for a moment, take a seat, and rock in the warmth of a Spring's evening.

As I drive out through the country areas of Alamance County, I roll down the windows. No reason exists to be in a hurry because on a Spring evening, many friends and family sit on the front porch to rock away the last hours of the day. I throw up my hand to wave and even pull up in a driveway or two just to check on the residents.

"How's your week going?" I ask, sure that the concern of a neighbor and pastor means something to them.

"We're doing good. Beautiful weather we're having," a common response I hear on these nights. Every time, an invitation is extended for me to come and rock on the porch alongside them. Some nights I do.

Other nights, I refrain so I can check in on a few more people.

What you notice is that on that porch, whatever they're facing, for a few minutes, it's set aside for the joy of relaxation. Stress gives way to a peacefulness, moments of enjoying a breeze, and the simple joy of saying hello to passersby.

Those moments are sacred. Children play in the yard as parents and grandparents watch from the porch. Laughter fills the air. Work is finished for the day. Bills wait until the morning. For at least a few moments, we unwind with those we love. There is a peace that comes as we rock on the porch.

Just as those moments of Spring offer us a break from all of life's stresses, Jesus offers us a relief as well, a refuge when we are overwhelmed. The heaviness of this life lifts when we accept His call to come. He opens His arms without condition. He calls us to a place where we can find the peace we so desperately need.

Weary and heavy-laden, we long for at least a moment to lay aside the weight of all we carry.

The Prince of Peace called and with the call, He offers rest. Inviting is the release of control, to lay aside the burden and allow Jesus to carry those burdens. Rest rejuvenates a weary soul and reenergizes a life running on empty.

Has life become so much that we have neglected to get away for a few moments? Are we too dialed in to situations that we've become unable to dial it down?

Spring calls us out to the porch for a season of relief. The rocking chair offers a reprieve, a place to find solace if but for a few moments on any given night. There's a place to go and let go.

plant the Word—

"Come to Me, all of you who are weary and burdened, and I will give you rest. All of you, take up My yoke and learn from Me, because I am gentle and humble in heart, and you will find rest for yourselves." (Matthew 11:28-29, CSB)

pray the Word—

Almighty Father, teach us how to lay the burdens of this life down and find rest in You. Remind us of the necessity of rest and draw us to Jesus where we find rest for our souls. Thank you for bearing the weight for us so that we can sit down and breathe.

work the Word—

We say we don't have enough time to unwind, but we cannot afford to neglect it. Take a stroll as evening comes. Sit beside a waterfall five minutes longer. Rock on the front porch. Do these activities and speak a verse of Scripture you've committed to heart. Give up what binds you as the Lord handles our issues even better than we do.

DID YOU KNOW?

The largest rocking chair in the United States is found in Casey, IL. The rocker stands at over fifty-six feet tall.

missed OPPORTUNITIES

THOUGH I WAS BORN AND RAISED A HOOSIER, WE LIVED IN FORT WORTH FOR A DECADE, AND I WILL NEVER FORGET THAT FIRST TEXAS SPRING. BEAUTIFUL BLUEBONNETS LINED THE HIGHWAYS AND BYWAYS. IT WAS BREATHTAKING!

I commented on the gorgeous wildflowers one day when I was chatting with my neighbor, and she quickly pulled out her phone to show me a darling picture of her daughter when she was about the age of my girls. She was sitting in a field of bluebonnets, wearing a bonnet, smiling the cheesiest of grins. Best picture ever! At that moment, I decided we, too, would have a photoshoot in the bountiful bluebonnets. I could hardly wait!

I bought the girls matching sundresses that coordinated with the purplish blue hue of the bluebonnets, and I also found the most adorable coordinating hats. I figured even if I couldn't convince Abby and Ally to wear the hats, they'd make great props in the pictures. Then I researched online to find out the peak week for bluebonnets in our area. I wanted to get it just right.

But here's the thing about bluebonnets: They're only around for a short time. They start blooming at the end of March, and usually they're all gone by the end of April. That particular spring, our schedule was jam-packed with the girls' competitive cheer practices and competitions, my work obligations, church commitments, and all of the other "stuff" that seem to fill up our days. By the time we were ready to take pictures, the bluebonnets weren't in bloom anymore. We missed our opportunity.

Thankfully, we got another chance for those dreamy pictures the next spring. But it was an important lesson for me and one that I haven't forgotten: don't become so busy that you overlook life's beautiful opportunities.

We missed out on something really great because we were so focused on our to-do lists and jam-packed calendars. It made me wonder, what else had we ignored while we were so preoccupied?

How many family dinners, honest conversations, walks in the park, and opportunities to make memories with loved ones had we missed?

Today, I challenge you to make room in your schedule and your heart for life's beautiful opportunities. Let's not let our opportunities from God go by. Let's act on His promptings when He nudges us.

Though the bluebonnets arrive every spring, some opportunities are lost forever if you don't act on them, so act! Seize the day! Enjoy the moment!

"Life's like bluebonnets in the spring. We're only here for a little while. It's beautiful and bittersweet."

AARON WATSON

plant the Word—

"Look carefully then how you walk, not as unwise but as wise, making the best use of the time, because the days are evil." (Ephesians 5:15–16, ESV)

pray the Word—

Lord, open my eyes to the opportunities that You have placed before me today. Help me to keep my focus on important things and help me to learn to say "no" to the things that You never intended for me to do. I love You. Amen.

work the Word—

Take a few minutes to examine your calendar or planner for the coming days. Are your days too full to experience things that matter to you? See if you can remove or reschedule some busywork to make room for opportunities closer to your heart. Ask God to help you prioritize your days. He's really great with time management. (After all, He created the world in less than a week.)

DID YOU KNOW?

Texas was the first state to plant flowers—bluebonnets being the main ones—along the side of the highway.

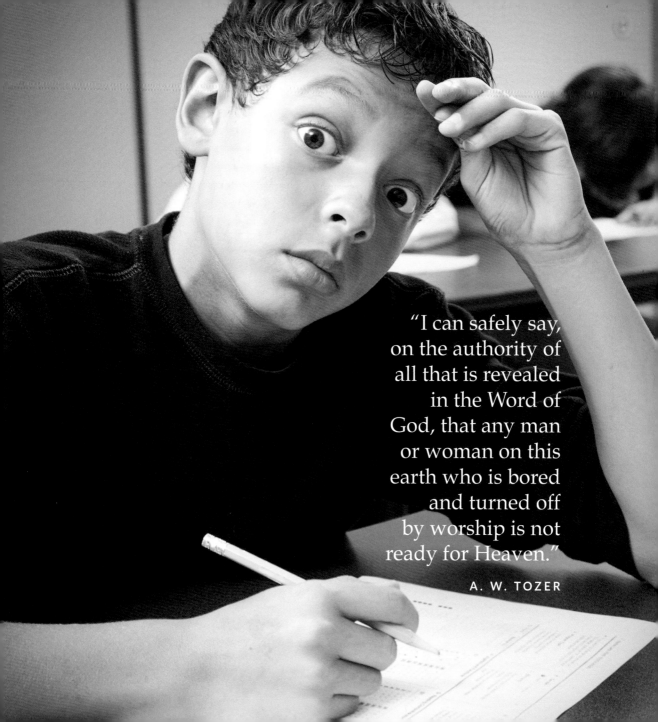

"I can safely say, on the authority of all that is revealed in the Word of God, that any man or woman on this earth who is bored and turned off by worship is not ready for Heaven."

A. W. TOZER

it's the finals COUNTDOWN

THE SPRING SEMESTER IN SCHOOLS THROUGHOUT THE NATION CULMINATES IN A WORD THAT STRIKES FEAR INTO EVERY STUDENT—FINALS. A WEEK OF STRESS, LONG NIGHTS OF CRAM SESSIONS STUDYING, AND ANXIETY MARKS MOST STUDENTS AS THE SPRING SEMESTER WINDS DOWN.

Even decades removed, we remember those days. We feel for the students enduring the rigorous testing now. Everything rode on those exams. Grades in high school affected college options. Grades in college dictated advancement or retaking a course.

One of the worst I endured came in college. In "The Life and Teachings of Jesus" course, the final exam consisted of forty verses from the gospels (Matthew, Mark, Luke, and John). We had to identify which gospel the verse came from and explain why we thought it came from that particular gospel.

I studied like no other time in my life. My face remained embedded in the gospels when I learned what the exam held. There are certain "tells" in the wording that reveals their origin, but without knowing it, you were simply making an educated guess.

When the day came, I excelled by the grace of God. The studying paid off.

"Great job," my professor told me later.

"I studied like never before," I assured him, the words anything but an over exaggeration.

He smiled. "It paid off. You were ready when the time came." He continued down the hall, but his words carried further than the Henderson Building at Mount Olive College.

I was ready for that test. My grades were a result of the work and time invested. But "ready when the time came" echoed in my ears on a deeper level.

Are we ready? When this life comes to a close, are we prepared for the moment? With exams, we knew when we had to be ready. The schedule told us long before that on a certain day, we had to take a test. But life offers no set schedule.

Our very existence on this earth is not guaranteed beyond the minute we are living right now. If it ends tonight, are we ready? Can we give an account for what we've done, the choices we've made, the life we lived?

Paul says that we should constantly examine ourselves. His direction to us was to delve deeper inside ourselves to see where we stand with the Lord. Have we died to who we were to live for Him? We say we're followers of Jesus but are we truly following Him? Paul set a baseline for the reader for the self-examination. He said we need to ensure we are inside the will of God.

This life will end, but we do not know when. A daily exam ensures that when this life is over, we can stand before the Lord in assurance that we passed the test.

DID YOU KNOW?

Speaking of exams, Penn State reported that states spend over $1.7 billion every year on the standardized testing for students.

plant the Word—

"Test yourselves to see if you are in the faith. Examine yourselves. Or do you yourselves not recognize that Jesus Christ is in you?—unless you fail the test." (1 Corinthians 13:5, CSB)

pray the Word—

Dear Lord, open our eyes to see ourselves clearly. Return our focus on our lives, so that we are honestly evaluating where we are with You. Show us what needs to change. Help us to make those changes. Guide us to a place where we are completely inside Your will for our lives.

work the Word—

Make a faith examination for your life. Take inventory of the fruits of the Spirit in your life and evaluate where you struggle. Ask the Lord to help you produce the fruits that are lacking. Use Peter's growth verses (2 Peter 1:5-7) and work on those steps to growth in life and faith.

MICHELLE

hummingbird HOG

EVERY SPRING, WE HANG A HUMMINGBIRD FEEDER OUTSIDE OUR WINDOW. IT'S SO MUCH FUN WATCHING THE HUMMINGBIRDS HOVER AROUND IT, SIPPING THE SWEET SUGAR WATER WE PUT OUT FOR THEM.

This Spring, I couldn't wait to try out my new feeder that actually sticks onto the window so you can get up-close-and-personal with the cute, little hummingbirds. As I watched for tiny visitors at our new feeder, I finally spotted the first one on the second day of May!

He was black and white, very different from the brightly-colored ones we usually entertain. I kept waiting for more hummingbirds to show up, but it was always the same little guy. Then I noticed that little black and white hummingbird (that I affectionately call "Buster") was pretty much camped out at our feeder. He flew around the area all day, but hardly ever took a drink. That's because he was too busy protecting his space and keeping the other hummingbirds away.

Whenever another hummingbird approached, he would chase it away by flying at it or even crashing into it! I couldn't believe it!

As it turns out, hummingbirds are very territorial. You wouldn't think with their tiny frames that they'd be so aggressive, but it's actually common for hummingbirds to fight for the right to a certain feeder or flower, especially if there aren't many feeding spots around. Hummingbirds need a lot of energy to keep flapping their wings that fast, so when they find a food source, they don't want to share it for fear that it might run out.

Buster was so preoccupied with keeping the feeder all to himself that he hardly ate anything at all. He was too stingy and self-absorbed to reap the benefits he would have enjoyed if he'd only shared his feeder. There was more than enough sugar water to go around, and I would've gladly refilled the feeder the moment it was low. But Buster was too afraid of missing out to take that chance.

Yep, we all have a little "hummingbird hog" in us. When we receive blessings, we aren't quick to share them. A lot of times, when we come into money, possessions, time, knowledge, or power (just to name a few), we see it as a scarce resource, so we feel that sharing it would make us weaker and more susceptible to danger. We can even get so caught up in trying to get as much as we can that we forget to enjoy what we already have.

"No one has ever become
poor by giving."

ANNE FRANK

That's not what God wants for us. We are meant to live generously, recognizing that everything we have is from God.

We are merely stewards of God's earth, so it is our responsibility to distribute its resources well. God rewards those who are good stewards. Many stories in the Bible show us that when you give more, you receive more—not only on Earth, but also in Heaven, where it is most important.

Let's not be like the hummingbird and keep the blessings we've found to ourselves. Let's share our resources freely and happily! Our Heavenly Father has more than enough to go around.

plant the Word

"The world of the generous gets larger and larger; the world of the stingy gets smaller and smaller." (Proverbs 11:24, MSG)

pray the Word

Lord, I thank You for the blessings You've given me. Please show me the places in my life where I've been stingy and help me to be more giving and loving like You. Lord, I trust You with all that I have. I love You. Amen.

work the Word

See if your church hosts a ministry fair. If so, attend and pray that God would reveal a way for you to be generous. If not, why not be the person to start one?

DID YOU KNOW?
Research from Harvard Business School shows that giving money actually feels better than using it for yourself. It makes sense. The Word of God says, "It is more blessed to give than to receive." (Acts 20:35, NIV)

"If I had stopped asking questions, that's where I would have remained."

LEE STROBEL

ANDY

getting rid of
THE CRABGRASS

SUN AND RAIN, WARMER TEMPERATURES, AND THE CHANGING OF THE SEASONS BRINGS THE ONCE DEAD YARD BACK TO LIFE.

A vibrant green overtakes the drab brownness that dominated the previous three to four months. Many take the time to work their lawns into pristine patches of perfect greenery.

We tried. Honestly, we made a valiant effort.

But, oh, the crabgrass! It grew everywhere.

I tried pulling it up to begin with, barely making a dent in the issue the first year. When I tore away the crabgrass, I planted new grass seed in its place. I lugged the seed bag from place to place around the yard and then religiously watered the areas of new seed. It was exhausting.

As the winter drew nearer, we assumed the crabgrass would die and we could get a fresh start the next Spring. What I learned later was that, with the death of the crabgrass, thousands of seeds fell in the yard. As Spring emerged the next year, more crabgrass appeared.

I finally turned to a friend who specialized in lawn maintenance and beautification.

"You tried to pull it all up . . . by hand?" he asked, trying to suppress the laughter at my attempt to solve the problem on my own.

"Yep. I didn't realize how long that would take. Then, I thought it would die out over the winter?" I explained.

"Well, it does, but it can multiply."

"So, I've noticed," I responded, a bit embarrassed at my lack of knowledge in the area.

He stepped back for a second. "Why didn't you just ask? I could have sprayed it and took care of it! You do realize this is what I do for a living," he commented, his very choice of words a revelation of the wasted effort on my part.

"I didn't want to bother you."

He proceeded to take care of the issue. Where crabgrass once grew, now beautiful grass emerged. I couldn't believe the transformation we saw that Spring. I wasted time and resources that could have been utilized for something else if only I had gone to the expert first.

Psalm 19 shows the importance of running to the expert in life. Left to our own understanding and our solutions in life, we struggle. Confusion sets in as the voices of others in our same position offer their advice. Our minds race as we seek to "figure things out". David knew where to go. As he penned Psalm 19, he pointed the reader where to turn for better results.

David knew that the Lord's instructions were the path to a renewal of life and that the Lord's Word offered an abundance of wisdom, even to the most inexperienced soul. Rather than attempt to do it alone, he turned to the Lord to know how to do it the right way.

Our lives tend to be a series of quests for answers. Too often, only after we exhaust everything and everyone else, we at last turn to the Expert, the Lord. His understanding exceeds ours and His solutions to all life presents are perfect. How does a transformation of our life begin? By allowing the Lord to transform all we are, to expertly weed out the world as He guides us closer to Him.

plant the Word—

"The instruction of the Lord is perfect, renewing one's life; the testimony of the Lord is trustworthy, making the inexperienced wise. The precepts of the Lord are right, making the heart glad; the command of the Lord is radiant, making the eyes light up." (Psalm 19:7-8, CSB)

pray the Word—

Heavenly Father, guide us to life through Your Word. Draw our attention to You when we face the unknown. Give us the wisdom we need each day and we ask that You transform our lives every day. May You be the One we turn to first when we need help, rather than using You as a last resort. Amen.

work the Word—

A dear friend of mine jokingly said to me one Wednesday night, "Why pray when you can worry?" The words hit home. Our faith tells us that God not only listens but that He knows all that we do not know. Start each day by praying for His guidance, understanding, and wisdom to be there as you go through the day.

God, the designer of life, is an expert in the field of life. He isn't too busy. He doesn't have too much to do. Amazingly, when we turn to the Lord, we save ourselves time, effort, and energy as we do things His way first rather than trying our ways first.

DID YOU KNOW?

According to Statista, the landscaping industry hauled in over 99 billion dollars in the United States in 2019.

MICHELLE

pretty LITTLE WEEDS

ONE AFTERNOON WHEN MY DAUGHTER, ABBY, WAS ABOUT THREE, SHE DISCOVERED A PATCH OF PURPLE WEEDS GROWING IN THE MIDDLE OF MY BEAUTIFUL BEGONIAS. ABBY PICKED ONE OF THE WEEDS AND BROUGHT IT TO ME.

"Here, Mommy. I picked you a flower," she said, enthusiastically.

I smiled and graciously accepted it. As I looked at the weed more closely, I thought, "My, this weed really is lovely. It could almost fool anybody into thinking it's a flower."

There are some weeds that look pretty, but make no mistake, they are an invasive species. They choke out the life of everything else in the yard. My friend Bethany and her family have recently moved from Florida to Virginia, which obviously has completely different foliage.

As they were tending to their new yard, and clearing out sticks and dead bushes, Bethany soon realized she had no idea which plants to keep, and which ones to uproot. All of the flowering plants along the fence line were pretty, but after doing some research and talking with the neighbors, she learned that most of those "pretty plants" were actually just "pretty weeds."

Many things in our lives can disguise themselves as flowers when in actuality, they are pretty weeds. Sneaky weeds. The hottest new binge-worthy Netflix series, a piece of juicy conversation about a friend, a hip slang phrase, or a questionable night out, can all seem like attractive things at first glance. But closer examination might reveal that you've stumbled upon a pretty weed that needs to be thrown out of your life before it starts growing roots.

The little weed that Abby proudly gave me all those years ago, looked so innocent and pretty among my begonias. But it would have eventually choked the life right out of them if I hadn't weeded my flowerbed. The same would've happened to Bethany's new yard if she hadn't cleared out all of the pretty weeds and replaced them with actual plants. And, if we continue to let little weeds of sin or darkness grow in our lives, they'll soon overtake us, too. That's how Satan tries to fool Believers.

So, don't be fooled by his tricks. Ask the Holy Spirit to reveal those "pretty weeds" so that you can extract them from your life.

The big, ugly weeds are easy to identify. It's the attractive ones we have to worry about. Let God be the ultimate Gardener in your life. As you live close to Him, you'll become more skilled at identifying the weeds in your life—even the pretty ones.

"You cannot take the mild approach to the weeds in your mental garden. You have got to hate weeds enough to kill them. Weeds are not something you handle; weeds are something you devastate."

JIM ROHN

plant the Word—

"There is a way that appears to be right, but in the end it leads to death." (Proverbs 14:12, NIV)

pray the Word—

God, please reveal the weeds in my life. Point out what I need to extract from my life and help me to remove them in order to make room for the good things You have for me. Amen.

work the Word—

Someone once said, "What you compromise to keep, you ultimately lose." That's so true, especially where our spiritual lives are concerned. The moment we start compromising our beliefs and allowing "little sins" to creep into our lives, our hearts are on their way to becoming less sensitive to the Holy Spirit's promptings, and we're on our way to becoming disconnected from God. The Word says, "They are darkened in their understanding, alienated from the life of God because of the ignorance that is in them, due to their hardness of heart." (Ephesians 4:18, ESV) Pray that God would help you stand firm in your beliefs no matter what, and that you'll be able to resist the urge to compromise any area of your life that would adversely affect your walk with God.

DID YOU KNOW?

Weeds cause more crop loss than insects, rodents, birds, or disease.

"We are all faced with a series of great opportunities brilliantly disguised as impossible situations."

CHUCK SWINDOLL

ANDY

a diploma,
A DEGREE, A WALK
ACROSS THE STAGE

GRADUATION DAY SPARKS CELEBRATIONS IN HOUSEHOLDS ACROSS THE GLOBE. WHETHER IT BE FROM HIGH SCHOOL OR COLLEGE, THE ACCOMPLISHMENT IS COMMEMORATED WITH A WALK ACROSS THE STAGE, A PARTY, GIFTS, AND AN ABUNDANCE OF PICTURES TAKEN.

When we graduate high school, our friends and families sit at football stadiums or in large auditoriums. We go and walk with our friends, the guys and girls we grew up with, some that we've known since the first day of kindergarten.

In college, some go, and others choose to sit out of the festivities. College graduations feature large classes of graduates, so many choose to sit out. When I graduated from Mount Olive College, I decided to sit it out. Unfortunately, the decision was not mine to make.

"When is graduation?" my mother asked.

"I don't know. I'm not going."

She looked at me with the look children understand. It was the moment when I thought I had a voice but the words that came from me were the wrong answer.

"Oh, yes you are," she responded.

"Mom, they will mail the degree to me. I don't want to waste a Saturday driving all that way and then driving all the way back."

"You are going. We are all going. We worked too hard for you not to be there."

As you can guess, we went. I walked across the stage. Mom snapped at least a hundred pictures and we went home afterwards. The day at Alumni Hall on the campus of Mount Olive showed that all the work, all the sacrifices, and all the stress had not been in vain. A degree proved achievement.

Graduation day always proves that the work was worth it. One of the most disheartening experiences of life is to work hard but have nothing to show for it.

Of all that we do in life, one thing offers us guaranteed fulfillment. Paul told the Galatians that there would be a payoff for the hard work one does for the Lord. As results may not come immediately, it was crucial that they kept pressing forward and doing right.

The good works of the believers needed to continue so that the lost world could be impacted. Just as a freshman's labor takes multiple years to lead to a degree, so the work of the Lord can take time to produce results.

But a reward will come. There will be a harvest later.

Don't give up. The struggle now leads to rejoicing later. The good work you are doing now will produce in something to show for it.

plant the Word—

"So we must not get tired of doing good, for we will reap at the proper time if we don't give up." (Galatians 6:9, CSB)

pray the Word—

Heavenly Father, push us forward even when forward seems to amount to little in the moment. Open our eyes to see how You are moving, what You are doing, and the way You take our efforts and create a harvest. Father, we need Your encouragement today and we need Your hand to bless the efforts of our lives.

work the Word—

See the way God has blessed efforts in your past. See how the little things we do in the name of Jesus have been used in bigger ways than we imagined. Make a list and make a reminder to yourself to never stop doing what is right.

DID YOU KNOW?
The percentage of graduates of private colleges and universities exceed the graduates of public institutions. According to *What to Become,* 33.3 percent graduate in four years in public colleges while 52.8 percent do so in private institutions.

ANDY

it's
ON FIRE

A DAY OFF IN THE SPRING OPENED THE DOOR TO COMPLETE TASKS I HAD NO TIME FOR EARLIER. MANY OF THE TREES SHED THEIR LEAVES LATE IN THE WINTER, SO WHEN THE SPRING ROLLS AROUND, IT'S TIME TO BURN OFF LAST YEAR'S REMNANTS TO CLEAR THE WAY FOR A NEW YEAR.

As I set out to burn the leaves, my wife surveyed the work. Her eyes scanned the location I had chosen, which in retrospect was a terrible choice.

"Do you think you need a fire extinguisher?" she asked, her question underlined with the suggestion that I did, in fact, need one.

"No," I replied with a sigh. "I'm standing right here. If it gets out, I can put it out quickly. Plus, there isn't any wind today. I've got this."

"Okay . . . if you say so," she scoffed as she turned to go inside.

I waited for her to get into the house before I began mumbling to myself.

"'Do you need a fire extinguisher?' I'm not an idiot," I groaned as I moved more leaves to the burning pile.

Out of the corner of my eye, I saw the Christmas tree from the previous Christmas. It seemed like a natural time to get rid of it as I was already burning leaves, so I dragged the brown corpse of a once beautiful green tree and tossed it on the top.

Flames shot into the air. I scurried to retrieve the water hose because I was scared. I stood ready to douse the flames and thankfully, they died down to a more manageable height after a minute. As I stood there, heart beating out of my chest, I heard a knock on the sliding glass door. I looked over to see my wife, a fire extinguisher in hand, smiling and mouthing to me, "Do you think you need this?"

The flames died down and we died laughing that night. The fire consumed what was needed to be consumed that day even if it came with a moment of panic.

On the day of Pentecost, a fire broke out. Tongues of flames fell on the disciples and the Word spread quickly to those in Jerusalem. Thousands heard and believed. So engulfed were they by the Spirit that they immersed themselves in the flames. They listened to the teaching. They ate together. They prayed together. Pretty soon, what began in Jerusalem spread beyond. The disciples moved as the Spirit moved and the gospel accomplished what needed to be done.

Moments of fear arose. Some even tried to extinguish the fire raging from the day of Pentecost. But the

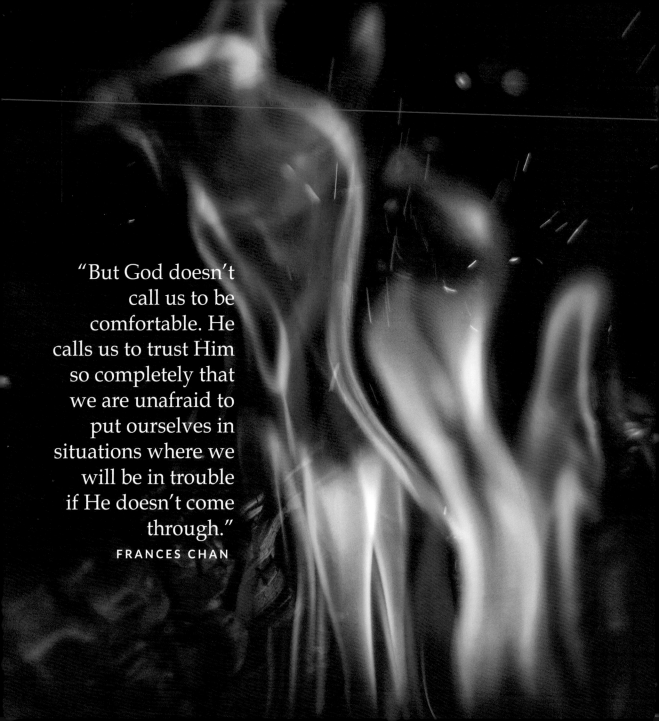

"But God doesn't call us to be comfortable. He calls us to trust Him so completely that we are unafraid to put ourselves in situations where we will be in trouble if He doesn't come through."

FRANCES CHAN

Lord kept it burning and the fire continues to burn throughout the world today. A passion for Jesus sweeps through the land today.

Paul warned us not to stifle the Spirit. Rather than extinguish the fire, we are to fan the flames. Though it may appear to some as a cause for concern, the gospel consumes us for the glory of God. Don't be afraid. Let Jesus stoke the flame.

plant the Word—

"Don't stifle the Spirit." (1 Thessalonians 5:19, CSB)

pray the Word—

Heavenly Father, create a fire in us. As Your Word says, You are a consuming fire, and we ask that You consume our lives today. We need You. We long to burn for You in this day and in this season. Let the fire begin in us so that it might spread to others.

work the Word—

Find what sets your soul on fire and use it. For some, there are specific worship songs that drive them to a more passionate worship. For others, certain Bible passages engulf their soul like nothing else. When you feel a fire for Christ burning in your life, do not allow anything to put that flame out. Stoke it. Share it.

DID YOU KNOW?

According to *Discover* magazine, Earth is the only planet on which fire can burn. The reason is that only Earth offers enough oxygen to keep a fire burning.

"To fall in love with God is the greatest romance; to seek Him the greatest adventure; to find Him, the greatest human achievement."

SAINT AUGUSTINE

MICHELLE

mockingbird MAYHEM

THE MOCKINGBIRD IS ONE NOISY GUY. I MEAN, HE SINGS HIS LOUD—VERY LOUD—SONG ALL NIGHT LONG. I KNOW BECAUSE THERE'S A MOCKINGBIRD THAT LIVES NEAR OUR HOUSE, AND FROM MIDNIGHT TO 5 A.M., HE'S OUTSIDE MY BEDROOM WINDOW SINGING HIS LITTLE HEART OUT.

After several restless nights, I had to wonder why he sang while all of the other birds were sleeping. Like, what's the deal? Everybody else is trying to get some shut-eye!

So, I did some research, and I discovered that it's the bachelor mockingbirds who give those nightly serenades in hopes of attracting a potential mate. I sure hope the mockingbird outside our bedroom window finds his Mrs. Mockingbird soon so I can get some sleep! I'm a city girl, and now that we live on the edge of the woods, I'm still learning to love the sounds of nature. The songs of the mockingbird? Not so much.

Research has shown that male mockingbirds sing long and hard in desperate hopes of attracting a mate. My noise complaints aside, it's sort of romantic, really.

Night after night, he sings. He knows what he wants, and he will do whatever it takes to get that mate's attention.

We should be just as passionate about pursuing our relationship with the Lord. Would we be willing to sing all night to find Him? Would we call out to Him, night after night, seeking His companionship?

Many of us can't even bother to dust off the Bible long enough to read a chapter or two every day. We become too busy, too bored, or too tired. We give up too easily.

But the Bible says that we will find God when we seek Him. All we have to do is show up and put in the effort. Like the mockingbird who stays up all night crooning for his mate until he finally finds that special female companion, we should be willing to put in the time it takes to develop a close relationship with our Heavenly Father.

DID YOU KNOW?
Mockingbirds, which are known for their ability to "mock" other noises, have been known to mimic several hundred different noises, including other birds, frogs, and even human music and machinery.

plant the Word—

"I love those who love me, and those who seek me find me." (Proverbs 8:17, NIV)

pray the Word—

Lord, here I am. I want to be with You; I want to hear Your voice; I want to know You. I will not stop calling out to You, even when I can't yet sense Your presence, because I know You are here. I love You, God. Amen.

work the Word—

Today, spend some extra time reading the Bible, praying, and listening to worship music. By "extra," I mean more than you usually spend on any given day. Maybe that's five minutes, or maybe it's an hour. Just push to pursue your relationship with God a little more than usual. You'll discover the more time you spend with Him, the more time you'll want to spend with Him.

a gift that
KEEPS GIVING

PUSH-MOWING A YARD PROVIDES GOOD EXERCISE BUT ALSO DRAGS OUT A DAY. FOR YEARS, I HAVE USED A PUSH-MOWER IN OUR YARD. FROM START TO FINISH, THE EFFORT TOOK A LITTLE OVER TWO HOURS, BUT THAT DOESN'T INCLUDE THE HOURS OF DREAD LEADING UP TO MOWING THE YARD.

There were times when I hired others to mow just so I didn't have to do it myself.

All of that changed with a gift. Crystal's grandparents moved and no longer needed their riding mower. The generosity of their hearts led them to give us the mower even though they easily could have made a great deal of money by selling it.

"I hope you will enjoy it," Papa said as he delivered it to our house. He smiled wide, knowing I would appreciate the tool to make mowing faster.

"You made my life so much easier," I told him as I admired the orange machine.

Papa taught me what I needed to know about the mower. Though the mowing season had ended a few weeks earlier, I looked forward to the next year.

During the next spring, the grass rose up. As I mowed one evening, one by one my kids came out to sit on my lap and drive the mower around the yard. I taught them how to steer and throughout it all, they laughed and begged to take one more lap. Brady smiled as we turned and twisted throughout the front yard.

A task once dreaded became something to enjoy, moments to share with my children.

Papa's gift changed my outlook and changed something I didn't want to do into something I long to do. The moans of aggravation gave way to shouts of excitement in our home, all because of the gift we were given.

David shared a similar transition in his life, only it was on a much grander scale. David looked at the life he lived but saw how the gifts of God turned his sorrows into shouts of praise. What God gives changes our entire outlook on life.

David begins Psalm 30 by praising the name of the Lord, then gives the reasons. He said that God lifted him up, protected him, and gave favor to David.

God's greatest gift to us is salvation through Jesus Christ. Salvation reminds us that even the most sufferable parts of life are endurable, because something greater awaits. His presence, a gift unto itself, brings us to a place of praise because we are not going it alone in life. Favor from the Lord promises that our needs will be taken care of by the

"All these people, all these
things came into my life,
and they're all blessings
from God. And now that
I look back, I realize that
these are His fingerprints
all over my story."

JEREMY LIN

Giver of all good things. Our Lord stands as the Gift who continues to give.

Our lives are blessed because of the blessings of God. When we stop and look at what He has done for us and what He is doing for us, our frustration gives way to shouting of praise because of the gifts He provides each day.

plant the Word—

"You turned my lament into dancing; You removed my sackcloth and clothed me with gladness, so that I can sing to You and not be silent. Lord my God, I will praise You forever." (Psalm 30:11-12, CSB)

pray the Word—

Father, help me to see all the blessings You provide in my life. What I take for granted, show me how You provide it. Keep praise on my lips as You raise my awareness of all You have done.

work the Word—

List the blessings of your life. When you think of one that has not made the list, add it. Keep a rolling list of what God has done for you and you will see how much you grow in your thankfulness for Him.

DID YOU KNOW?

House Method conducted research on the amount of time people spend mowing their lawn. Depending on where you live and the manner in which you mow, one person could spend up to forty-seven days of their life mowing grass.

"Perseverance — that was the key word then, and it still remains the basic principle for anyone who wants success. You cannot creatively get anywhere in this life without sturdy application of the persistence principle."

DR. NORMAN VINCENT PEALE

MICHELLE

persistence
PAYS OFF

WE RECENTLY MOVED TO A HOUSE THAT BACKS UP TO A COUPLE OF ACRES OF WOODS BRIMMING WITH WILDLIFE. AS SOMEONE WHO HAS LIVED IN TOWN MY ENTIRE LIFE, THIS IS QUITE A LOVELY CHANGE. DEER. BIRDS—ALL KINDS OF BIRDS. FROGS. RABBITS. CHIPMUNKS. IT'S LIKE WILD KINGDOM HERE!

But you know what I love watching the most? Our adorable squirrels. We have gray squirrels and fox squirrels who come to visit us every day. I realize they're actually coming for the birdseed but it feels very personal, as if they know me.

I love watching these determined little squirrels. No matter what kind of feeder we put out, even those guaranteed to be "squirrel proof," the squirrels figure out a way to get the birdseed. They are clever, but more than anything, they are persistent. They will hang by their tails and swing or stretch as far as their bodies are capable of stretching in order to scarf down a few sunflower seeds.

Even though I have two squirrel feeders stocked with corn for their taking, they apparently prefer the black oil sunflower seeds and they work hard to get them.

Some of my bird-loving friends don't share my love of squirrels and are quite annoyed by their constant pursuit of the birdseed intended only for birds, not squirrels. But I feel quite differently. In fact, I think the acrobatic squirrels have earned the right to gobble up the birdseed, so I refill my feeders often, and I will continue to do so.

You know, as I watch these determined squirrels, I wonder how much further along I'd be in my walk with God if I were as persistent in seeking God, and as diligent to consume His Word, as they are to eat that birdseed.

Sure, I have my quiet time with God, but there's a difference in having your time with God and being hungry for it. I intend to be more like my squirrel friends when it comes to diligently seeking what I want the most in life, and that's a closer relationship with God.

So, when is the last time you truly craved spending time with your heavenly Father? Have you been diligently seeking Him?

DID YOU KNOW?
The word "seek" appears in the Bible (KJV) 244 times. It's true!

plant the Word—

"Seek the LORD and His strength; Seek His face evermore!" (1 Chronicles 16:11, NKJV)

pray the Word—

Father, help me to crave Your Word even more than the squirrels crave birdseed. Help me, God, to put You and Your Word first in my life, and please help me to find quality time to spend with You. Thank You, Lord, for loving me and being so patient with me. I love You. Amen.

work the Word—

Proverbs 8:17. NIV, says, "I love those who love me, and those who seek me find me." What a great promise! God promises in His Word that if we seek Him, we will find Him. I find it interesting that this verse uses the word "seek" instead of "look." "Looking" is a much more passive activity, but "seeking" means you're deliberately searching, and that's the kind of seeking God desires from us.

HERE ARE A FEW TIPS TO GET YOU INTO THAT SEEKING MODE.

1. Set a time of day and choose a place where you'll read the Bible each day. Why not wake up 30 minutes early and go to your favorite place in the house? Maybe it's the window bench in your bedroom or that comfy chair in the sunroom. No matter the time or location, just get a plan and spend some time with God before jumping into your day.

2. If you're new to having a quiet time with God, or maybe you've never spent much time reading the Bible, a good place to start is in the four Gospels—Matthew, Mark, Luke, and John. Also, I like to read a Psalm or a Proverb each day.

3. Many people like to read through the Bible every year, and there are many systems for accomplishing that feat. Go to biblestudytools.com to peruse several different plans.

ANDY

wish i may,
WISH I MIGHT

THEIR EYES SCAN THE FRONT YARD EVERY TIME WE STEP OUTSIDE DURING THE SPRING. A TREASURE AWAITS IF THEY FIND IT FIRST.

What is the adventure awaiting? What outdoor offering creates the urge to search far and wide?

"There's one," Cheyenne calls out, running to the right to retrieve the object.

"I see one," Autumn exclaims as she runs forward, plucking hers from the front yard.

Crystal and I watch the scene unfold. The girls grab theirs, shut their eyes for a second and utter a wish, then blow each piece off the stem of the weed they pulled.

"Look to see if there's more," Cheyenne instructs.

Inevitably, we meander down to the hill in the front yard. Typically, a smattering of those have grown since the last time I tackled the yard with a mower.

With each one, they repeat the steps. A few minutes and a few "wishing flowers" bring joy to their little faces. These "weeds" are actually dandelion seed heads, but they are only known as wishing flowers at our house.

Every time, I attempt to trick the girls into telling me what they wished for before they blew the wishing flower, dispersing the seeds.

"If we tell you, our wishes won't come true," they explain, serious about their intention to conceal what they wished for moments earlier. Throughout the Spring, this scene unfolds in our yard, priceless moments with our children.

They pin at least a little hope on the legend of the flower. They invest something in the hopes of a favorable outcome.

Aren't we glad that we have a more effective way to receive what we need in life? As believers, we don't need the power of a wish because we believe in the power of prayer. When we call upon the name of the Lord, we are beckoning the Lord of creation to intervene. When we pray, we must believe that God hears the petitions of His people.

Do we believe God hears? Do we trust that He will answer? Too many times, we treat prayers like nothing more than a wish. But a prayer is so much more.

James says that a prayer should be prayed from an expectant heart. The one praying believes God can and trusts that God will.

Don't ask because you've got nothing to lose. Approach the Lord knowing there's everything to gain when He hears our prayers and acts. He's proven Himself worthy of our confidence.

plant the Word—

"Now if any of you lacks wisdom, he should ask God, who gives to all generously and without criticizing, and it will be given to him. But let him ask in faith without doubting. For the doubter is like the surging sea, driven and tossed by the wind." (James 1:5-6, CSB)

pray the Word—

Heavenly father, remind us of all the prayers we've offered up that You've answered. Give us glimpses of Your power so we turn to You first with the confidence that You can do all things. Thank You for hearing us. Thank You for helping us.

work the Word—

Keep a prayer journal. List the answered prayers of your past. Ask friends, family, and church members about the prayers they had answered and allow it to increase your faith today.

DID YOU KNOW?

The wishing flower holds dandelion seeds. According to All American Turf Beauty, the seeds can be carried away up to five miles from where they originate.

"The more you pray, the less you'll panic."

RICK WARREN

"True prayer is a way of life,
not just for use in cases of
emergency. Make it a habit,
and when the need arises,
you will be in practice."

BILLY GRAHAM

MICHELLE

bathing suit
SEASON #GYMTIME

I'M CONVINCED THERE'S NOTHING PEOPLE DREAD MORE THAN PUTTING ON A BATHING SUIT AFTER A LONG WINTER OF LIVING IN COMFORTABLE LAYERS OF CLOTHING.

Let's face it, trying on a bathing suit can be a real shocker if that long winter included lots of Christmas-cookie munching and hot-chocolate-with-marshmallows sipping.

That's why when the weather starts hinting at warmer days, people start hitting the gym in droves. Seriously, you can't find an available cardio machine in the entire gym.

As a longtime fitness instructor, I always knew my January cardio and strength training classes would be completely full all the way up until Spring Break, and then . . . not so much. Without the impending need to fit into a bathing suit for a Spring Break beach vacay, the determination and drive to get fit disappeared. Suddenly, the gym parking lot cleared out, my classes dropped in numbers, and cardio machines became readily available.

We often do the same thing when it comes to prayer.

Many of us only turn to God in seasons of necessity, when we need a "quick fix" to get through the current crisis. In other words, we don't spend any time in prayer until we find ourselves in need of immediate intervention from Almighty God. But when the crisis is over, we start talking to God less, and we put Him on standby until we need another quick fix. Sound familiar?

Maybe you have prayed desperately about a pressing situation in your life, and then once it was resolved, you ignored God until the next crisis. I'm guilty of it, too.

The Bible tells us that God is a jealous God (Exodus 34:14), meaning that He doesn't want you to put anything above Him. God wants to spend time with you.

He desires a personal relationship with His children, and in order to have that kind of relationship, we need to talk to Him on a regular basis—not just when we're in trouble.

In fact, we should long for Him, deeply desiring His presence, all the time. The more you read the Bible and get to know God, the more you'll desire His presence. You'll want to talk to Him every day—in good times and bad times—simply because He is your Heavenly Father.

Don't let prayer be a quick fix like hitting the gym before Spring Break—make it a powerful daily habit and start developing that personal relationship with your Heavenly Father.

plant the Word—

"As the deer pants for streams of water, so my soul pants for you, my God. My Soul thirsts for God, for the living God. When can I go and meet with God?" (Psalm 42:1–2, NIV)

pray the Word—

God, thank You for always being there for me. I want to invite You into my whole life. I love You and want to spend time with You, even when I don't need anything. I just want to be with You, God. Please nudge me throughout the day to spend a moment in prayer and put You first place in my life. Amen.

work the Word—

Say a prayer right now in which you don't ask for anything—just praise God and give thanks to Him. Spend time with Him. If it helps you, set up alarms on your phone throughout the day reminding you to pray, even if it's about nothing in particular.

DID YOU KNOW?
Ninety percent of people quit going to the gym after only three months.

let's go to
THE YARD SALE

YARDS TRANSFORM INTO OUTDOOR STORES AS SPRING OFFERS THE PERFECT WEATHER TO TAKE SPRING CLEANING TO A WHOLE NEW LEVEL. AS PEOPLE CLEAN THEIR HOMES, THEY CLEAR OUT SPACE BY GETTING RID OF THAT WHICH THEY NO LONGER USE.

People go shopping in the yards throughout the community, looking for a deal while enjoying the outdoors.

My cousin is an antique dealer and his mother, my aunt Shirley, is an antique collector. They understood yard sales better than most others because they studied antiques and could find treasures that others thought were nothing.

Early on Saturday mornings, they arose before the sun came up to visit yard sales near the Charlotte area.

"Why in the world do they get up so early?" I asked my mom as we discussed going with them one Saturday.

"You have to go early for antiques," she tried to explain, her insight still unable to motivate me to get up that early.

"I still don't get it."

"You have to go early if you're going to find any antiques. Other people are searching for antiques, so you have to be one of the first to get there. If you wait until eight or nine o'clock, the yard sales will be picked through and there won't be anything valuable."

I finally understood. As antiques were their passion and their business, they gladly arose early and raced from yard sale to yard sale. They discovered treasures that others just wanted to give away or get rid of. Their passion fueled their pursuit so that nothing stood in the way of their Saturday morning scramble.

Jesus taught parables about the kingdom of Heaven. In teaching the parables, He sought to help the audience understand how valuable heaven truly is. He told stories they understood. The parable of the treasure in the field illustrates it well. Upon finding the treasure, a man sold everything and bought the field containing the treasure. He understood what the field held and was willing to sell everything else to be able to possess the treasure. He sacrificed what he had to embrace what he could gain. A passion for what he found inside led to his purchase of the entire field.

What will you give up for the kingdom of Heaven? Will you give up sleep to find the treasure and will you sell all you have to embrace something bigger? Is there a passion inside you for the treasure of Jesus?

"The kingdom of Heaven is worth infinitely more than the cost of discipleship, and those who know where the treasure lies joyfully abandon everything else to secure it."

D. A. CARSON

Giving up a little of this world, sacrificing a little sleep, and giving up some time is all worth it if we give up those things in a passionate pursuit of the kingdom. How hard are you pursuing God today and do you see the value of the kingdom of Heaven? Such a pursuit pays off.

plant the Word–

"The kingdom of Heaven is like treasure, buried in a field, that a man found and reburied. Then in joy he goes and sells everything he has and buys that field. Again, the kingdom of Heaven is like a merchant in search of fine pearls. When he found one priceless pearl, he went and sold everything he had, and bought it." (Matthew 13:44-45, CSB)

pray the Word–

Lord, You are the treasure of our lives. Give us the wisdom to value the kingdom of Heaven above all else. What this world offers is nothing compared to the value of Heaven. Give us the drive to pursue the kingdom with every ounce of energy we have in this life.

work the Word–

One of the ways we change the pursuits in our lives is to weigh the value in that which we are pursuing. Go through the activities and hobbies of your life and assess a value of each one. Remember that church and the Bible are priceless. When you look at the television or a computer screen, or your phone, remember that what it holds is not as valuable as spending time pursuing the kingdom of Heaven.

DID YOU KNOW?

According to Alliance Work Partners, Saturdays are the best day to host a yard sale and each week, an average of 95,000 sales are listed on Craigslist.

"We will stand amazed to see the topside of the tapestry and how God beautifully embroidered each circumstance into a pattern for our good and His glory."

JONI EARECKSON TADA

MICHELLE

beauty FROM MESSES

SOME THINGS NEED EXTRA CAUTION. CARRYING A CUP OF STEAMING HOT COFFEE REQUIRES ONE'S FULL ATTENTION TO AVOID THE PAIN OF BURNING ONE'S HANDS WITH THE SLIGHTEST SPILL.

Transporting glass from one destination to another is a cause for caution and anxiety. Filling up bird feeders with sunflower seeds, however, never seemed to be an activity where extreme caution was needed.

My husband, Jeff, would disagree.

You see, every time I feed the birds, inevitably, a little seed falls to the ground no matter how careful I am. Yes, I'm a bit messy but I always justify the spilled seed, knowing it won't go to waste. The chipmunks and the squirrels enjoy the sunflower seeds on the ground.

Last year, an amazing thing happened. Out of my mess, God produced a beautiful surprise. Apparently, one of those sunflower seeds fell in the right location. Before long, that seed took root and eventually, a big, beautiful sunflower appeared. Every time I glanced out the window and saw the sunflower stretching toward the sky, I was reminded of my Father's goodness and His ability to take my mess and produce something lovely.

God has a way of doing that. He takes the messes that we make in life and from that, He creates beauty.

The Bible is filled with stories of messiness becoming beauty over time. Saul's life was a mess but on the road to Damascus, he met the Lord, and that encounter changed his name and his life. Think about the woman caught in adultery. A mess came to the feet of Jesus, but forgiveness found its way to her, along with a new life and a new beginning. Finally, the ugliness of the cross comes to mind. Barely recognizable as a human, Jesus hung there and died an ugly death, yet out of that death, we were given a beautiful opportunity to spend eternity with Him.

Life presents messes. Some seasons are messier than others. But in the middle of it all, God can produce something beautiful.

You may not be able to see it yet, but just like my glorious sunflower, after just a little while in the ground, that seed will burst forth in beauty. Your life will do the same.

DID YOU KNOW?

Young sunflowers track the sun from the beginning of the day until the end. According to ScienceMag.org, the face of a sunflower moves throughout the day to face the sun. We should do the same with the S O N.

plant the Word—

"The Spirit of the Lord God is on Me, because the Lord has anointed Me to bring good news to the poor. He has sent Me to heal the brokenhearted, to proclaim liberty to the captives and freedom to the prisoners; to proclaim the year of the Lord's favor, and the day of our God's vengeance; to comfort all who mourn, to provide for those who mourn in Zion; to give them a crown of beauty instead of ashes, festive oil instead of mourning, and splendid clothes instead of despair. And they will be called righteous trees, planted by the Lord to glorify Him." (Isaiah 61:1-3, HCSB)

pray the Word—

Father, through the mess, show us how You can bless things in life. We call upon Your hand to work amid the scattered, to bring about beauty from the mess and from the overlooked in this life. Plant that which reminds us of You with every turn in our lives. Amen.

work the Word—

Take a moment today and reflect on how God has turned past messes into beauty in your life.

ANDY

oh! those cool, REFRESHING WATERS

TEMPERATURES RISE. AS THIS SEASON ADVANCES, WARMTH INCREASES AND BEFORE LONG, THE BEADS OF SWEAT FORM, LEAVING US LONGING FOR SOMETHING REFRESHING.

In the Spring of 1987, we had a specific place we visited for water. Even over thirty years later, I think about that spring when I drive by that way.

My family decided to take a bicycle trip to the Outer Banks of North Carolina. To prepare, we spent over a year training, riding a little further every week as we sought to get our bodies into shape.

By the spring, we pedaled from our house to Chapel Hill, a total journey of sixty miles. Though the hilly terrain took its toll on us physically, one stop highlighted each journey to college town.

"Pull into that church," my dad instructed us as we reached the Spring Friends Meeting House.

The old, white, wooden church has an impressive history. The first meeting of the church took place before the Revolutionary War. Our purpose for stopping, however, poured out of the ground near the edge of the church property.

"Grab your water bottles," he instructed.

All four of us made our way down to a ditch. Out of the hill cascaded a natural spring. The coldest water ran forth. Each of us drank from the fountain and refilled our water bottles for the rest of the journey.

Something about that water reinvigorated us. Even more inspiring was that we had to pass that spring again on the ride back home. Again, we stopped. The water refreshed us again.

Recently, I drove back to the place. The water continues to run and is as cool as I remember it being back in those days.

A lady walked to the well in the heat of the day. Most visited the well early in the morning, before the intense heat, but this woman had a reputation. Rather than face the shame and the stares of others, she waited until everyone else finished. As she approached one afternoon, there sat Jesus at the well.

He offered her living water. The well would quench her thirst for a moment, but what He promised was living water, able to quench a deeper thirst forever. Her soul thirsted for more than what she previously drew from the well and what she found in life. Who she met at the well promised to satisfy the soul.

Living water flows from the same place today. Jesus is the well that never runs dry. The living water He gives rejuvenates the weariest soul. Dried land finds the rain needed, the life dehydrated by the world becomes a fountain of living water in Him.

"The living water passages
tell us we become vessels for
God to pour Himself into so
we can pour him into others."

MARK HALL (CASTING CROWNS)

As the nature of life takes away, a stop at the well of Living Water fills us up again. Are you thirsting for more in life today? Is your soul parched? Come to the place where the water flows endlessly, where refreshing and replenishing never runs dry. Come to the fountain that is Jesus.

plant the Word—

"But whoever drinks from the water I give him will never get thirsty again—ever! In fact, the water I will give him will become a well of water springing up within him for eternal life." (John 4:14-15, CSB)

pray the Word—

Dear Lord, remind us that when we thirst for more, we can come to the fountain and find what we need. We thank You for the living water that is Jesus. We ask that You create a spring of living water in us today.

work the Word—

Medical professionals insist that we drink a certain amount of water each day. Here is a good habit to get into starting now. Read John 4:14-15 each time you get a glass of water and commit the verse to your memory. As a result, glasses of water become biblical reminders and even gospel opportunities.

"Listen in silence,
because if your heart
is full of other things,
you cannot hear the
voice of God."

MOTHER THERESA

MICHELLE

peeping
PEEPERS

HAVE YOU EVER HEARD A PEEPER? I HAVE. IN FACT, I HEAR THEM JUST ABOUT EVERY NIGHT BECAUSE THEY HAVE BEEN LIVING IN THE SWIMMING POOL OF THE HOME WE'RE REMODELING. THEY'RE LITTLE FROGS WITH A BIG SOUND.

Their "song" is very distinctive and can be almost deafening when a plethora of peepers are present. (If you're not familiar with their nightly noise, go to YouTube and search for "peeping peepers" and have a listen.) Their chorus is kind of cool, even if a bit mind-numbing when it goes on all night.

Now that I've heard the peepers' distinct voice, I'd recognize it anywhere, even with all of the other sounds of nature competing for my attention. That got me thinking about hearing God's voice. Do we recognize His voice in the noisy world we live in? Do we hear His distinctive voice and know it's Him? Or does the chaos around us drown out His whispers in our hearts?

I think a lot of times, when we feel lost, it's because we've lost track of God's voice. We can't hear Him over the sounds of notifications, conversations, televisions, and the worries running through our heads. We aren't sure whether we're pursuing something because God is leading us or simply because we heard about it on social media.

The solution? Spend some quality time alone with God on a regular basis. Just like you recognize your best friend's voice having listened to it so much, you'll begin to recognize God's voice when you continually hear it through scripture and prayer.

We all need dedicated time when we are only listening to God. Not our phones, not our televisions, and not even our loved ones—just God and His Word. Over time, this helps us distinguish His words from the words of those around us.

Just like those little peeper frogs with their distinctive melody, God has a certain way of talking to our hearts. Once you've "heard" Him, you'll begin to know His voice and hear His direction above all of the other noises in our world. So go ahead. Unplug from the world and plug into Your Heavenly Father.

DID YOU KNOW?
A peeper's famous peeping noise comes from the air being squeezed out of its lungs into an inflatable vocal sac on its throat.

plant the Word

"My sheep listen to my voice; I know them, and they follow me." (John 10:27, NIV)

pray the Word

Lord, clear the noise in my world and in my heart so I can hear what You have to say. Help me to become better at distinguishing Your voice over all of the other voices in my world. I love You. Amen.

work the Word

Schedule a time on your calendar to have complete alone time. Let your loved ones know that you will be unavailable and go somewhere quiet. Whether it's five minutes or a few hours, focus in on seeking God's voice in scripture and prayer. Grab a journal and a pen and begin what some people call "a listening journal." Here's how it works.

YOU GET ALONE WITH GOD AND PRAY. THEN, WRITE DOWN A SIMPLE, SPECIFIC QUESTION, SUCH AS:

"God, what do you call me?"

Then, I look through the scriptures and write down those answers. For example:

*I am a child of God: "But to all who have received him—those who believe in his name—he has given the right to become God's children." (John 1:12, NET)

*I am a friend of God: "I no longer call you slaves, because the slave does not understand what his master is doing. But I have called you friends, because I have revealed to you everything I heard from my Father." (John 15:15, NET)

Then, I ask God, what do you call me, specifically, Father? Listen for His answer and write in your journal the impressions you feel/hear. This is a great way to practice hearing from God.

though it's SPRING HERE, AUTUMN COMES ELSEWHERE

WE FEEL THE CHANGE, AND IT IS GOOD. A SEASON OF BITTER COLD GIVES WAY TO THE WARMTH WE'VE LONGED FOR SINCE THE END OF THE PREVIOUS YEAR. WE'VE ENDURED THE DARK AND THE COLD, NOW THE HIBERNATION IS OVER, AND SPRING DRAWS US OUTSIDE AGAIN.

Spring provides hope and joy. The warmer temperatures and the longer days speak to the soul just as the new growth around us inspires us. People smile bigger, spend more time together, and express a thankfulness. Winter's harshness grips us no longer. Spring has sprung us free.

However, a different transition takes place on the Southern Hemisphere. The warmth of summer gives way to the chill of fall. Winter looms on the horizon, and each day, the warmth escapes a little more.

Rarely do we think about the seasons outside of where we live. Spring amazes us with its beauty and rebirth. We enter six months of warmth and festiveness. The future is bright as we approach a positive turn in conditions and elements. Outside of meteorologists or those with family members in other parts of the world, we don't think of what the people in the Southern Hemisphere are experiencing.

The warmest months here in the United States coincide with the snowiest months in the Southern Hemisphere. The southern island of New Zealand and the mountains of Chile experience the bluster of the cold and the effects of snowy precipitation. Our turn towards better weather in the spring means they are inching closer to worsened conditions.

Much like we fail to think of the seasonal changes in other parts of the world, we can fail to see the seasons of someone else's life right beside us.

Our lives know struggle and push us on a daily basis. It becomes easy to focus on the current season of our lives without thinking of what others may be enduring.

The story of the Good Samaritan illustrates this truth so well. A man is beaten, robbed, and lying on the road. Priests and Levites pass by, unmoved by the beaten man's condition. They had lives to live. There were places to go and things to get done. The Samaritan, however, stopped even though he had places to go as well. He saw the man and considered his condition.

Ecclesiastes provides the best insight on the shifting seasons in life. Solomon points out the extremes. Just as there is an appointed moment to be born, there will be a moment that ends in death. Today

"The risk they run from famine fever and smallpox is not slight, but, no doubt, they have counted the cost and are ready to lay down their lives, as others have done in previous famines."

ANNIE ARMSTRONG

may bring weeping while tomorrow might provide laughter. Some seasons are pleasant while others are marked by the struggles.

See beyond the season of your life today. Look for those who are in a season of struggle and reach out to them. Find someone in a season of blessing and rejoice. Never get so wrapped up in your own season that you fail to see that you can be important in the season someone else is currently enduring.

plant the Word—

"There is an occasion for everything and a time for every activity under Heaven: a time to give birth and a time to die; a time to plant and a time to uproot." (Ecclesiastes 3:1-2, CSB)

pray the Word—

Heavenly Father, give up the eyes that see beyond our own situation to realize the season others are in. Let us rejoice with those who are rejoicing and send us to weep with those who are in a season of sorrow. Use us to help others through the season they are in today.

work the Word—

Listen for the insight of what others are experiencing. If you hear someone talking about a struggle in their life, find a way to make an impact. Send them an encouraging text. Make a meal for a family who lost a loved one. Make time to go into a nursing home and spend time with people who are lonely.

DID YOU KNOW?

The Annie Armstrong Offering, taken up during the Easter season each year, took in over $62 million in 2019, a record high contribution for missionaries to reach people with the gospel.

about the
AUTHORS

Michelle Medlock Adams is a *New York Times* bestselling ghostwriter and an award-winning journalist and author of more than 100 books including *Dinosaur Devotions*. Michelle is married to her high school sweetheart, Jeff, and they have two married daughters and five adorable grandchildren. Learn more at: www.michellemedlockadams.com.

Photo by Richardson Studio

Andy Clapp is an award-winning author and pastor. Andy's debut novel, *Midnight, Christmas Eve*, released in 2021. Andy is married to Crystal and they live in North Carolina, along with their three children: Cheyenne, Autumn, and Brady. Learn more about Andy by visiting www.andyclapp.org.

Photo by Jaime L. Pike Photography